THE BEST OF BOTH WORLDS

JOHN ANDREW

WILLIAM B. EERDMANS PUBLISHING COMPANY
GRAND RAPIDS, MICHIGAN

ISBN 0-8028-3689-5

To †Michael and Joan Ramsey

Contents

Contents

Acknowledgments

I have again Cheryl Steiner to thank for so painstakingly typing into manuscript form the sermons and addresses that form this book. My own handwriting is a challenge not merely to colleagues and friends but to myself at times, and Cheryl's patient and persevering deciphering has earned my admiration and the envy of others who have to struggle with it.

Again I must pay tribute to those who have had to sit and listen: priest-colleagues, my parish family, the many visitors who throng St. Thomas Fifth Avenue. And last but not least, the choristers. Who gives much thought to these invaluable servants of the Lord, both big and little, who have to sit still and appear to listen, twice a Sunday in the full view of the congregation? It so happens that over forty youngsters of school age, cassocked, ruffed, and surpliced, sit on those hard choir stall benches, and twelve professional singers behind them, not all of whom are Anglicans, for a start. Their marvelous courtesy and friendliness make my job even more pleasurable. I owe them all a great debt for their cheerfulness and cooperation. Our choristers raise the worship to the heights with their sublime music, and that makes the task of preaching easier.

Who says that the day of the sermon is over? I am not alone in thinking that a constituency can be built of thoughtful, seeking, critical people hungry for God's Word to be divided and his claims articulated. I acknowledge their faithful persistence.

Sam Eerdmans, my friend in the publishing house that produces this book, is the source of encouragement and timely reminders to be up and doing. I value that. And need it.

Finally, I need to acknowledge the strength that the friendship of Bishop Michael Marshall affords me. A superb evangelist himself, he is honored in this place where his frequent visits bring strong Christian and godly sustenance.

Time and again there is the necessity to ponder the words of holy women and men who love the Scriptures and write so tellingly about God's loving dealings with us in Christ. William Barclay is one such, as is Austin Farrer, and the great William Temple. Of Archbishop Michael Ramsey I can only speak in terms of filial love and undying gratitude . . .

J. A.

Preface

You will have noticed that this book is dedicated to two people, one dead and one alive, whom I have loved over two-thirds of my life. To Michael Ramsey I owe everything in my priesthood. He not only made me deacon at his first ordination in York after being enthroned as archbishop some days previously; he also taught me all I know theologically. People know that were I ever to have an entry in *Who's Who,* I would put against my education, "educ: by Michael Ramsey Archbishop of Canterbury, after Oxford." He taught me priesthood, too, just by showing how he wielded his. He taught me manners, because he was very old-fashioned in his courtesies to people, and I needed to learn from him. He taught me to try to be accurate in how I expressed things, and I have come to see that that was the most valuable of lessons. His mind was orderly and *clear.* I loved it.

And then Joan, Lady Ramsey, his wife. She enchanted me when first I met her, over thirty-five years ago. We have been friends long over thirty years. Her wit and intelligence, her writing style, her extraordinary gift of hospitality, her elegance, and her faith have all been integrated into one amusing and beloved character. I have laughed with her as with no one else, ever. Through world travels, through desperate sickness, through exhaustion, and through exhilaration she has been a steady friend, an admired wife and partner of my Employer (as I used to call him), and an honest, at times devastating, critic. You need not reach for the saltcellar with Joan. Assessment of human foibles, humorously and accurately delivered with a smile, difficult situations laughed out of — to be with her has been one of the joys of my life. What a pair they made!

The sermons in this book were all preached in St. Thomas Fifth Avenue, New York, to the congregation that for eighteen years now has been my family and my joy. I am deeply proud of them for their critical loyalty to what we preach and teach and encourage them to do. They are a demanding lot. They have every right to be. We demand a lot of them. We try with the highest liturgical and musical standards that we can possibly reach (thanks to two genius colleagues, Fr. Gary Fertig, the vicar, and Dr. Gerre Hancock, the organist and master of choristers) to bring the parish family to the gate of heaven. It is a never-ending, back-breaking, glorious if sweaty enterprise to keep the pressure on, to let nothing fall between the cracks in our care for the individual worshiper and our concern for the Christian evangelism and outreach that flow from the worship we offer, when we try to do something beautiful for God.

They respond with surprising energy. Far from being a passive, detached, and dilatory crowd, they enthusiastically sing, make friends with newcomers, bring strangers in with them, and bravely participate in all sorts of strategies to alleviate want, welcome people hitherto untouched by the gospel, and sink their many differences of outlook and background and political loyalties and ethnic preferences as they come together. Manhattan is not merely a melting pot; it is a *crucible*. It is tough to live in, stay in, keep sane in, keep friends in. They try hard. And against daunting odds, their success rate is deeply moving and a cause for profound gratitude to God. I am impressed with people's goodness here. There is virtually no small-mindedness, not much judgmentalism. There *is* a lot of gossip, which on occasion irritates me. But this family of mine constantly conjures from me more than I imagine I can offer and effort more than I think I am capable of. Of this all my colleagues, both lay and clerical, would themselves bear witness in their own lives.

The title I chose for the book, *The Best of Both Worlds*, is to my mind the joyful affirmation of our redemption in Christ Jesus, our justification by faith, as St. Paul would have us claim, and our desire for the parish family to be Christ-centered. Christians *do* have the best of both worlds, which, when you consider it, are one. Everyone and all things are one in Christ Jesus, for heaven reaches from the next world into this with his life lived in us: "Nevertheless I live, yet not I, but it is Christ who lives in me." St. Paul understands and teaches this concept with great power and persuasiveness. It is indeed the best of both worlds.

Foreword

J ohn Gerald Barton Andrew, D.D., is a perfectionist if ever there breathed such a man. One cannot but be amazed at the energy, creative and imaginative, demanding and physical, with which he tackles every challenge, duty, and chore. Be it the designing of a new liturgy, the planning of a special occasion, the practicing of the precentor's singing for evensong, or the preaching of a sermon, his effort is perfectly and intensely focused, for he will accept nothing less than his very best at any and all times and places. His best, it must be said, is spectacularly good — *the* best, in fact. If he is rightfully and righteously exacting of his staff, he is even more exacting of himself.

For example, how many archbishops and bishops, archdeacons and deacons, precentors and, yes, rectors do we know who insist on rehearsing each versicle before every sung service, choral or congregational? Fr. Andrew is one of the precious few I have known in my career, and, for this and many other reasons, I consider myself the luckiest organist and choir director in the entire Anglican communion, not to mention these continental United States of America. He and I view our work together as a partnership, out of which has grown a deep and affectionate friendship.

Imagine then, given his gifts of industry, intellect, and imagination, how compelling his sermons are. I have had the great good fortune to have worked with Fr. Andrew for nineteen years, and I have heard him preach many times, but not often enough.

I always *learn* from his sermons; how often I have marveled to hear one of the major canticles explicated and made clear to me, the layman.

I always *enjoy* his sermons, for he engages our imagination at the very outset of the sermon, with either an amusing observation or an intriguing story. His reverence for the English language, its written and spoken diction, is marvelous.

I am always *inspired* by his sermons. His articulate expression of the gospel's meanings to us all is a revelation and, at times, even a discomforting one, bringing us to reflect and rethink.

I am always *helped* by his sermons. He may not always give us the answers we feel we need, but he always leads us along the way toward our Lord, the source of all answers. You see, he cares so much, as do all true pastors.

With this volume, we are in for a wonderful series of treats. Read, learn, enjoy, be inspired and helped by one of Christendom's most gifted — and generous — preachers.

GERRE HANCOCK, Doc. Mus.
Organist and Master of Choristers
St. Thomas Church Fifth Avenue
New York City
Ash Wednesday 1991

A Word about the Place

Some years ago in Britain a book, *The Parish Comes Alive,* was published. It was difficult for the rector's predecessor to draw any other inference than that his successor, the author, had found the parish dead when he got there.

I realize that the first thing I want to do is to pay tribute to my wonderful predecessor, a man of high intelligence and learning and a devoted priest and preacher. So I could only say in my prayers of gratitude to God for him and for what he had allowed me to inherit that "Thou hast set my feet in a large room."

A large room it was. Could ever a church have a luckier location than St. Thomas Fifth Avenue, on a midtown corner opposite a subway station, with the whole world passing its doors the whole waking day? And then, a jewel of a building, beautiful outside, staggeringly lovely inside, the joyous, generous response of all New York to a spectacular act of recklessness by Ernest Stires, the rector in 1906 after the previous building had burned. *All* the money collected for its restoration, the insurance as well, some $1,200,000 in total, was wired to the victims of the San Francisco earthquake the day after the disaster. Within ten days, impressed New Yorkers had thrown a greater sum into the kitty. Earlier restoration plans were scrapped, and architects Bertram Goodhue and Ralph Adams Cram were brought in. We are the inheritors of their masterpiece.

This, plus the unique seventy-year-old foundation of the St. Thomas Choir School with about forty-five boys as boarders providing a choir of exceptional potential; a remarkable organist and master of choristers, Gerre Hancock, himself with his wife deeply committed to Christ and the church; and an endowment that the generosity of families of earlier days had provided were the givens in the challenge facing a young rector from the Church of England.

The challenge was simply this: to use all that we had been given in an attempt to make Christ's reality known in this part of New York City. With all the limitations I had to acknowledge about myself, I realized that if the claims of Christ were presented cogently, intelligently, and courteously in a setting of worship as fine as we could achieve, people might listen and respond. That this has happened in a quite remarkable way we acknowledge with thanksgiving to a loving Lord whose Spirit has breathed mightily over this place. I think it is true that my principal colleague, the vicar of this parish, and I have never really been satisfied with the standards we try to achieve. Always we find ourselves pushing for better worship — hymns carefully chosen with tunes that people can sing whether old or new (if they're new, then the rector takes the congregation into his confidence and asks them to sing a couple of verses before the liturgy, so that when the hymn has its turn they are not surprised or resentful), the Holy Scriptures provided in the pews for the congregation to use as they follow the readings, readers trained to read, liturgy beginning on the stroke of the hour, service leaflets carefully scanned for mistake or omission — all these things and more that have to be done and that take an enormous amount of time. The rewards of this are that people love to come and come in great numbers, week in, week out.

I made reference to the Bibles in the pews. I am a firm believer in biblical literacy. Laypeople should be knowledgeable in the content of God's Word. On Sundays before the great liturgy at eleven there is the Rector's Forum, a forty-five-minute Bible study, preparing the class for the Scriptures set aside that day for the liturgy. In Advent and Lent we have intensive Bible courses, and this year we are planning an additional midweek Bible class.

Leadership is in the hands of the laity. I am forever saying that it is the laity who are the evangelists, the clergy who are the encouragers and the friends of all on board each particular committee. So the chairmanship of each committee is in the hands of a layperson, and I assign one of the clergy to be a chaplain to every organization. The clergy are not the policymakers; they merely sit in to welcome, to encourage, to reassure, and, if asked, to advise. Of the three daily eucharists, the first and the last begin with morning and evening prayer, always recited by laypeople, women and men, who later serve the eucharist and administer the chalice. They read the Old Testament lessons in the great liturgy at eleven on Sundays. A group of three or four from the vestry help the rector out as a "ministries subcommittee" to whom hopefuls come when they say they feel called to the priesthood. If their peers recommend them wholeheartedly to the rector, their names are sent to the Ministries Commission of the Diocese. The impetus brought by the imaginative and hard-working people of all ages in a city as diverse as New York to the enterprise of evangelism is felt by the great congregation as a whole. It has been said that we are the fastest growing parish in the diocese, one sadly not known for its numerical expansion. From every possible economic, ethnic, political, and denominational background these people come, filling the church with families and single folk, old and young, the unknown and the famous, the very poor and those who have lives blessed with prosperity. Their generosity staggers me, their humor refreshes me, their forgiveness strengthens me and all of us who make many mistakes as we try to get things right for God. And they sing! The sheer volume of song and spoken acclaim is as bracing as it is surprising. And after it all, there is much friendly exchange and a great deal of work for the clergy as they try to "work the crowd."

If you get the worship right, the chances are you will get everything else right. It is curious but true that people's needs assume a clarity and urgency far keener with souls lifted up in worship. You can well imagine the extent of homelessness, poverty, depravity, and evil that abound in this enormous city. As we have nothing to offer by way of shelter to the homeless, we make sure that existing shelters for the homeless get all we can afford to give them. And we give them a great deal. Some of you may remember the world premiere of Andrew Lloyd Webber's *Requiem* on national television. We sent the entire proceeds from that premiere to the Church of the Holy Apostles' Soup Kitchen — in addition to what we already pledged to it and to many institutions like it. Our people visit the old and shut-ins, distribute food in kitchens for the poor, conduct English classes for Hispanics, go as workers into the hospitals in lay chaplain programs, and run some of these programs. Work among alcoholics and dependents has increased to the extent that there are nineteens programs weekly here. A fine young priest is the chaplain to all this work, himself a recovering alcoholic whom God has blessed with great self-discipline and success in conquering the disease. We are entirely — I had almost written *hopelessly* — involved in the lives of the people who surround this place, and my hope is that there will be no end to our endeavors before there is an end to the need for them. Exciting, yes. Exhausting, yes. Frustrating, often. Joyful, immensely. Fulfilling, superbly. Our motto comes from the Psalms: "O God my heart is ready." My hope is that these words will be engraved upon every heart in this place.

For †Michael Ramsey
The One Hundredth Archbishop of Canterbury

When the king in *Alice in Wonderland* was asked where to begin, he said gravely, "Begin at the beginning, ... and go on till you come to the end: then stop." Begin at the beginning.

For a Christian the beginning is not where you might think it is. It is not the birth of Christ. It is not the teachings of Christ. It is not the cross of Christ. It is the resurrection of Christ. Listen:

> The Resurrection is a true starting-place for the study of the making and the meaning of the New Testament.
>
> We are tempted to believe that, although the Resurrection may be the climax of the Gospel, there is yet a Gospel that stands upon its own feet and may be understood and appreciated before we pass on to the Resurrection. The first disciples did not find it so. For them the Gospel without the Resurrection was not merely a Gospel without its final chapter: it was not a Gospel at all. Jesus Christ had, it is true, taught and done great things: but He did not allow the disciples to rest in these things. He led them on to paradox, perplexity and darkness; and there He left them. There too they would have remained, had He not been raised from death. But His Resurrection threw its own light backwards upon the death and the ministry that went before; it illuminated the paradoxes and disclosed the unity of His words and deeds. . . . It is therefore both historically and theologically necessary to

1

"begin with the Resurrection." For from it, in direct order of historical fact, there came Christian preaching, Christian worship, Christian belief.

A. M. Ramsey, *The Resurrection of Christ* (1945), p. 9.

In 1945, at the end of the Second World War in Europe, a young man wrote a book on the resurrection of Christ that was acclaimed a little masterpiece. He was forty-one, the age I was when I came to be rector here in 1972. Already *he* was distinguished as a scholar, a professor in an ancient and famous university, a canon of an ancient and famous cathedral, both in Durham, and his name was Arthur Michael Ramsey. I have just quoted from the opening pages of his book. And what better time of the year to quote it than in Eastertide?

Michael Ramsey, Lord Ramsey, the one hundredth Archbishop of Canterbury, went to God early yesterday morning, after a brief bout with bronchial pneumonia. His wife, Joan, had told me on Thursday that he was ill and dying. I could hear him coughing as I spoke to her. He would have been eighty-four in November.

It takes a mind of great breadth and depth to express deep truths about God simply. This was the gift God gave to Michael Ramsey. Michael used that gift to the end of his long life in teaching and preaching and writing. Thousands upon thousands have read what he wrote. Nobody could ever get hold of the wrong end of a stick about God from reading what he wrote. He was a sublime teacher, pellucid as crystal, brief to the point of sparsity, plainly worded, and masterly. He knew his theology — he knew it because he had prayed it. It came from hours of contemplation. In the years I worked for him at York and in Lambeth Palace, I would constantly discover him immobile, lost in thought, doing none of the productive things I'd hoped to get him to do. Letters waited. People waited. Decisions waited. Push him into saying something before he was ready and he would stutter and stammer and appear to dither. He earned much criticism and name-calling for that. But when he was ready, he could be devastating with his honesty and *un*common sense. Uncommon. It came from a dimension most were unaware of, many were totally unfamiliar with: the realm of the invisible God, where he spent much time. People who were in politics or public life for themselves, the self-promoters, the ambitious, and the big talkers of all political parties never understood his vocabulary, and he would never modify it to please them. They were furious when he turned his gaze upon what they were up to and stated the godly considerations in strategies they were involved in. He would never impute motive even when he might have had just cause: he thought that loathsome, and said so. But what he was, was rebuke enough.

Do you know where he discovered his vocation? Here, in this city. On 46th Street on the West Side. In the Church of St. Mary the Virgin. He went in one day as an undergraduate law student. He came out half an hour later knowing that he would hope to be a priest. He never turned away from that decision, and he turned his powerful mind to theology, the study of the Bible, the history of the church, the thought and doctrine of the church as Anglicanism taught it. He had the inestimable benefit of a nonconformist conscience. His father was a West Yorkshire Congregationalist. Michael was later, as Archbishop of York, to confirm his old father as an Anglican. The nonconformist conscience was shot through with English liberalism. His preferred option was always therefore with the poor, the underdog, the marginalized, the discriminated against.

The faith he taught was wired in the heavens and grounded in the little people, their distresses and their misfortunes, long before many people made much mention of

3

them. In this he stood squarely not merely among the non-conformists but among the Catholics of the Anglican persuasion — teachers, heroes, martyrs for the faith, whose undoubted prince and leader he was and whose saintly successor he became. That Catholicism of his was recognized in its authenticity by members of the European Roman Catholic community who placed his books as required reading in their seminaries and made him a Doctor of Sacred Learning in their universities. Never has there been an Anglican so well known and so much read and valued among the Catholic community on this planet. I watched him teach the Catholic faith in these places. I was at his side in Rome in 1966 as Pope Paul's guest when the Holy Father took off his ring and placed it upon Michael's finger as a symbol of recognition too daring even at this date to be imagined. I heard him teach Lutherans about Luther's theology in Germany, and Wesleyan Methodists about Wesley's theology in England, and Calvinists about Calvin's theology in Switzerland. Everywhere he went he could and would put the cloak of truth around his shoulders and people would recognize it as their own and thank God for him and his ability to wear it, to live it, and to impart it.

Plutocrats bored him. The self-satisfied maddened him. But give him a room full of students and he would be in his element. He would take them and their views seriously, would spend hours in discussion and debate, would send their professors packing in order to be left alone with young minds and loving souls. They could — and did — say anything to him, and he was unshockable, infinitely patient, always challenging. Give him a piece of Scripture to expound, and after a minute of thought he would start laying foundation stones of thought, building an edifice that his hearers could get inside and make their own.

The frontal we have with O GOD MY HEART IS READY was designed by me, using Michael's favorite confirmation text, a quotation from the Psalms. This great professor would come from his car in a tiny Yorkshire village on a cold November night to confirm, or to install a new priest. He preached his sermon many times from the same text. I once told him when he had laryngitis that if he would open and shut his mouth I could preach the confirmation sermon by heart. And I pretty well still could. His people revered this venerable head on a pair of footballer's shoulders, a halo of white hair and unruly eyebrows moving up and down like a windy sea. I was the son they never had. As his son, I knew him at his nastiest, and I would say he was a bit of a saint. Eccentric always, maddening at times, impossible to predict, aloof and engaged by turns, attentive and remote by turns, patient and impatient, humble beyond telling and sometimes inconsiderate and demanding, terrifyingly intelligent always, this holy man's mind was shaped by the resurrection about which he wrote so tellingly. Now he is experiencing the truth of it — my father, my teacher, my example, and my archbishop.

He is to be buried in Canterbury Cathedral next week, and I plan to be there with Joan his wife. All through this coming week we shall have eucharists for the repose of his saintly soul; next Wednesday, a great choral requiem at 12:10. We owe him this. The church throughout the world owes him this. He is, I know, content to have begun his journey as we rejoice in Christ's Eastertide, his pain laid aside, his vision cleared, and his voice raised in worship as he gazes upon the source of the love and light he taught us all so much about and about whom he already knew so much more than most of us. He will be saying, "O God, *now* my heart is ready, my heart is ready: I will sing and give praise with the best member that I have. For I am risen with you and free and well and strong to enjoy you for ever!"

The Cultural Captivity of the Church

There are not a few of you who have heard me say, "Give me time!" when they think that I ought to be up and doing something they deem important. It's often a defense mechanism, a plea to be given space to think a project or a strategy through. And that is absolutely necessary if you want to be wise. I know this and I admit it. But, like you, I have to admit something else I know: that there are and have been many occasions when time given was not time *used;* it was frittered away, wasted on other things and sometimes wasted while I was making busy-noises. If you are honest (and I haven't often doubted that you are honest), you can and will relate to what I've been saying. You have asked for time, demanded time, been afforded time, taken time, and not made the most of it, not used it up, not employed it for the purpose you took it. And it may possibly be that you have not only wasted *your* time but somebody else's as well. So the sin of waste can be a double sin, for which on occasions we are twice guilty.

Advent is supremely the season to think about this. It is the beginning of the church's year. It is the season to think and to plan. It is the season not for sleeping but for waking, not for wasting time, either your own or other people's, but for redeeming the time, not for relaxing but for readying. For at hand, we are reminded, at hand is the arrival of something of eternal significance that has to be prepared for. Prepare ye the way of the Lord! Arise! Shine! For thy light is come! The event of eternal significance is the vindication of Christ's sovereignty over everything upon the earth, the great day of the Lord, when his rule will be acknowledged and "every tongue confess that Jesus Christ is Lord, to the glory of God the Father," a time when man's stewardship shall cease, and the accounting for it begins, when all possessions will be seen in terms of a brief borrowing, when earthly power and prestige will no longer be thought to be an individual's private property, when human wisdom and knowledge and experience and expertise in manipulating nations by political theories will be weighed in the balance and their plausible truths found wanting, when history will be discovered to have been lopsided and inadequate and inaccurate if not downright misleading, when "the secrets of all hearts shall be disclosed," when

> Knowledge, hand in hand with peace
> shall walk the earth abroad;
> the day of perfect righteousness
> the promised day of God.

All that is not a threat. It is a promise. And we are told that we are the inheritors of that promise. We are involved, as fellow heirs, with big expectations. What the church has done to be faithful to her side of the promises is part of the accountability we must share as members. As I tried to say last week, it is no good pointing outside to "them," to the bishops, to the General Convention, to the decision makers and takers. It is us, here, ourselves. Before us this Advent is the consideration of "the tension for God's people . . . between the voice and wisdom of their own day in history and the calling of the culture of the kingdom that is beyond history and yet which breaks into history supremely in the coming of Jesus." We are wondering how far

7

the church of our day has capitulated to pressures to take to herself attitudes and assumptions that may distort or caricature the stern demands of the gospel inheritance of which she claims to be the guardian.

I am reminded that a text from St. Paul for this brief homily might not be out of place: I will quote it from two translations; the first, the King James Version of Paul's letter to the Romans, chapter 12 verse 2:

> Be not conformed to this world, but be ye transformed by the renewing of your mind.

The second translation is that of William Barclay:

> And do not shape your lives to meet the fleeting fashions of this world; but be transformed from it, by the renewal of your mind, until the very essence of your being is altered, so that, in your own life, you may prove that the will of God is good and well pleasing and perfect.

Paul is warning against *chameleonism:* matching the colors of whatever we're next to. If it were a consideration in the first century, it is no less a consideration now. Look at the Christian way of trying to look at God: as seen in a Trinity of persons, Father, Son, and Holy Spirit. The church hammered this concept into shape from what we can read in Scripture, from what Christ tells us of his Father and of the Holy Spirit, and from what he claims to be in relationship to his Father. The story of this hammering into shape takes many pages of early church history. People argued, they fought, and battles were not unknown as this concept was considered. Great thinkers among the early fathers of the church, as we call them, pondered long years of their lives to write what they did. Tertullian, schooled in his Latin way, wrote much about the relationship of Father, Son, and Holy Spirit in the Trinity and gave us insights into the divine love that interacts and focuses the work of the Trinity.

But to feminists the usual masculine attributions to two at least of the persons in the Trinity — namely, God the Father and God the Son — have been a source of irritation, and the pressure for inclusive language has been persistent enough for some to discard the descriptions of the early Fathers and to substitute for them three entirely new nomenclatures: the Creator, the Redeemer, and the Sanctifier. It sounds neat as a side-stepping device to avoid the Father/Son image. And it is a clever and able move as far as it goes. But some of us think that it doesn't go far enough. The titles Creator, Redeemer, Sanctifier overnarrow the work of the persons of the Trinity, ascribing to them roles that reduce their individual competence. I will take one example. To assign to the Father the title of Creator narrows our understanding of God. The experience and devotion of the church requires that we also recognize the presence and work at creation of the Son, as supported by Scripture, *and* the presence of the Spirit, who, Genesis tells us, "moved on the face of the waters" and who was thus equally and honorably part of the miracle of the creation as we understand it. In other words, you can't ration creation to only one person in the Trinity.

I have merely dipped one finger into this pool of debate. This is no time for a trinitarian lecture; I merely wanted to sketch a tiny corner of the canvas of speculation about an area of our worship of the one true and living God.

Attempts to define a doctrine of the Trinity are doomed to failure, for God's personality cannot be contained and enclosed in words. Moreover, words that seek to avoid inflammation in other areas of life are likely to be just as fallible as those that do irritate certain sensitivities, and they can be seriously misleading, as I think this feminist attempt to desex the Holy Trinity is.

This is not to deny the work of those who have helped us to awareness of the mothering aspects of the God who

9

loves us as "a hen gathers her chicks under her wings" (those are Christ's own words), for which I am not alone in profound gratitude. This area needs more and not less explanation, and more will be forthcoming. It *is* to warn the church that superficial acceptance of palatable language can be a capitulation to modern culture.

This then might well be an area the church needs to look to, for she is accountable — we are accountable — to Christ our king and our judge for the way we phrase our references to the triune Godhead, to whom all power and majesty are ascribed, for time and for eternity. Amen.

Seeing Straight

Some people are gifted with what is called second sight. It is the ability to detect without the benefit of much evidence the shape an event will take, the outcome of an incident just beginning, the fate of a project, the future of somebody's life. It is a gift not always on tap, not always available; the person who has it cannot constantly predict with accuracy every picture in the time frame. There are flashes of intuition — visitations, you might say, of a special awareness that may startle and trouble the person visited. I spoke with a man who described having a vision of this sort. He was having a conversation with his son one day when he had a vision of that son's death in an air crash — and it happened exactly like that within six weeks. You can imagine the horror of the father at the sudden sight of his son's destruction in his mind's eye, and the appalling desolation when the son's death was reported to him *six weeks later*.

And some people, rarer still, seem to have this second sight on command. There is the fascinating story in the Old Testament of King Saul visiting the witch of Endor. I suppose now we should call her a medium. He asked her to bring up the spirit of the prophet Samuel at a time in his life when things were going badly for him in his struggle with the Philistines. Saul asked her if the spirit of Samuel was visible to her. " 'What do you see?' And the woman said to Saul, 'I see a god coming up out of the earth.' He said to her, 'What is his appearance?' And she said, 'An old man is coming up; and he is wrapped in a robe.' And Saul knew that it was Samuel" (1 Sam. 28:13-14, RSV).

And he lives to regret his visit to the witch of Endor, for he hears things he does not want to hear about his campaign from the spirit of the old man wrapped mysteriously in a robe who had come up out of the earth. Remember that Saul, not the witch, had identified whatever it was that she saw. She didn't know who it was that appeared to her. Saul was left to come to terms with what he had asked for. He had made his bed and was told he must lie in it. In his case, it required two mysterious gifts of somebody entirely else to make him face his destiny, the shape of his life, the collapse of his hopes, the reality of his future given what he had made of himself. This troubling, unusual, occasional ability, second sight, however exercised and whenever — how this can be and why this should be is hard to explain. I can't explain it, nor can the people with this gift, I imagine. But it brings us up against a fact we ought to make allowances for: another dimension in our lives with views occasionally accessible to the human discernment across the time frame as we know it.

Then there is another kind of sight, much more common: hindsight. The psalmist had it when he said, "It is good for me that I have been in trouble; that therein I may learn thy statutes" (Psalm 119:71, BCP). That is rueful; so is his observation that "before I was troubled I went wrong, but now I have kept thy word" (Psalm 119:67, BCP). He had learned this lesson so well that he could even say that the experience he had suffered had done him good, and he was obviously going to think more than twice before he strayed from the straight and narrow. Once bitten, twice shy. The gift of hindsight is available to most of us, not simply to a certain few. It is easier to learn from your mistakes than to detect disaster for yourself or for others ahead along the road of life's path. Easier, though some never learn, even from hindsight. They never become wiser even if they become sadder.

But it is about the sight God has of us and we have of him that I am concerned with as we try to teach and preach the meaning of Advent for us. The word means "approach," the approach of God to us, the coming confrontation, the meeting, inevitable as it is, after we have been beckoned through death's threshold, and the doors have been shut behind us, and before we realize it almost, we look into the eyes of God. True it is that as Christians we have experienced one death, when we died with Christ in the waters of baptism, the drowning of the mere natural man to be given the breath of new life in Christ. There faces us the next baptism — Christ's own word for his death in Jerusalem — our departure from here to what Christ himself assures us is the hereafter, in his company, he having led the way and waiting for us to follow, yet not having left us for a single moment as he pleads our case to the Father, as he makes intercession for us, as the Bible says — and as he judges us, for he sees us as we are, and our judgment is involved in what we do with the love he has planted in our hearts.

The present is supremely important, therefore, for our destiny is eternal. What do we do with the love he bestows? Keep it for ourselves and those we like and prefer to have around us? Or shed it around and share it generously, broadmindedly, exercising the stiff muscles of our charity despite the inevitable aches? *Judgment.* Do we heave a sigh of relief, accepting his forgiveness as if it were our due, and then withhold ours from others who have sinned more grievously toward us? *Judgment.* Do we glorify him by realizing that his love for us is a mark of his deep reverence of *us*, or do we glorify ourselves and each other by forgetting that we ought to share his reverence with those very different from us by virtue of distance, color, preference, lifestyle, class, aptitude, talent, and temperament? *Judgment.* For how we view his love for us and how we dispense it is the test of the clear-sightedness we have of him. Let us not forget for a day or an hour that we are looked at by God.

Our view of God's requirements, of his demands, is crucially involved in our judgment, clouded as our view nevertheless usually is by our condition. For I suspect Paul had our last judgment in mind when he embedded the great hymn to love in the first letter he wrote to the church in Corinth — "Though I speak with the tongues of men and angels" (1 Cor. 13:1, KJV). Do you remember how he says, "for now we know in part, and we prophesy in part. But when that which is perfect is come, then that which is in part shall be done away. . . . For now we see as through a glass, darkly; but then face to face: now I know in part; but then shall I know even as also I am known" (1 Cor. 13:9-10, 12, KJV).

Paul talks of a mirror, not a window; of a reflection, not a view. You look, you see yourself. Encouraging or unnerving, it is the first step to self-realization. Over your shoulder another face appears. You may recognize it, but you see the truth only when you turn. Someone stands there in the mirror watching for the spark of recognition in your eyes, waiting and wanting to make himself known, and content (because he is humble) that you recognize him by reflection at this stage. His face is that of humanity. We might scowl at that face, sneer at that face, ignore it, dismiss it, lust for it, long to love it, pity it, suffer with it, or dare not look at it for shame, but the mirror is held steady. The hand that holds it is not yours. A glance reveals a nail-scarred hand. And in the other hand, keys. We can guess at whose face it is. A guess must suffice for now, for to turn from that mirror and look into the unreflected face is the turn we make on death's pillow a second before "our last and great awakening," when we shall know as we are known.

A guess must do. But a guess is enough. Paul tells us so. We shall know in part. Enough to make us see that there could be surprises in store in his judgment of us. For his love for us (which is, I guess, what all the divine judgment centers upon) is the greatest surprise of all. Our judgment has begun. The mirror is held by him before our eyes. The other face, the face of Christ hidden in the face of humanity, waits for recognition and for welcome in that mirror. And the hand that holds the keys rests on our shoulder. We turn — perhaps it may have to wait till after our last turn on death's pillow — to look at him in recognition, and then our look can change. He tells us to "look up," for our redemption draweth nigh, and then, in his infinite mercy which is his vengeance, please God, "when we awake up after his likeness we shall be satisfied with it."

Festival of Lessons and Carols 1984

High-sounding concepts in political speeches look threadbare from a distance. Claims to universal comradeship of the workers, for instance, get frayed around the edges when you look at the Gdansk shipyards in Poland and what happened there this month when workers remembered their comrades killed a few years ago, or when some miners from the British coal pits vote against the rulings of their national leaders. The truth is that you can corral people, get them under a banner on a parade, singing songs and shouting slogans, but at the end of the day they eat their suppers in their separate homes and individuality returns with every mouthful, personality reasserts itself, greedy or unselfish, gloomy or optimistic, grateful or ungrateful.

A philosophy or a political creed can't absorb the whole man, can't take all humanity in its embrace. What can? Love can. God knows love can. It is the one thing that can do it. His spirit fills this world. He is the love that makes the world not only go round, but go *on*. And we can know this for sure because of the event we gather to celebrate. Without fanfare, he comes himself to be with us, and to our surprise and sometimes to our confusion he makes his presence gently felt when simple people and the poor, like the shepherds, hear a baby cry. They are the first to discover him. Children are very often the only possession of the poor.

So he can belong to them as surely and as certainly as he can belong to us, with all we have been given and with all we enjoy. And in the least expected place and at the most inconvenient time, the whole of life as we envisage it and consider it best run is changed, in the twinkling of an eye. For love is disruptive and all-embracing at one and the same time. Its presence is an affront and an offense to hell-bent efficient materialism, direct and pushy selfishness. It gets in the way of forward-looking schemes for self-aggrandizement and it embarrasses self-justification just by being there. It wrecks projections from which God has been left out, getting under the feet of the proud and tripping them up. In the end it will wreak havoc with all totalitarian regimes. Love is here with us, and here to stay — the baby of Bethlehem, the despair of the slick, the hope of the poor, and the joy of the whole earth.

> Welcome, all wonders in one sight!
> Eternity shut in a span
> Summer in winter. Day in night.
> Heaven in earth, and God in man.
> Great little one, whose all-embracing birth
> Lifts earth to heaven, stoops heaven to earth.

Richard Crashaw (1613-1649)

Two's Company

Whoever it was that coined the phrase "Two's company, three's a crowd" had a problem on his hands. He verbalized for the human race the innate *resistance to hospitality* that lies in every human breast. The instinct to find somebody else to be loved by, to be cared for exclusively, wells up in every soul leaving childhood and a mother's warmth. When that search seems over, when two people have found each other, a love begins to grow from the attraction, and it can go one of two ways: it can be creative and expansive so that others feel its warmth and are strengthened by it, *or* it can become selfabsorbed, and three can be a crowd.

When this happens, there's trouble. Resistance to hospitality is one feature of the many stories we remember and celebrate in this magic Advent season. The classic occasion was the discovery that there was no room at the inn.

> Thou didst leave thy throne and thy kingly crown
>> When Thou camest to earth for me
> But in Bethlehem's home was there found no room
>> For thy holy nativity.

Emily E. S. Elliott (1835-1897)

Humankind is represented by the innkeeper who turned the little family from his doors and shut God out, leaving

18

Christ's mother only a filthy stable-cave to have her baby in, with its smell and its draughts and the mute acceptance of beasts of burden.

When you think of it, hospitality and resistance to it figured often in Christ's life. He loved hospitality — he made a country wedding into an unforgettable event when he provided his fellow guests with a heavenly vintage. He loved going to dinners with all sorts of people — many unsuitable, not that he cared. One might say that he was a pioneer in the area of fast food when he provided thousands with enough to eat and more from just five loaves and a few fishes. He got breakfast going for his friends when they came in from a fruitless fishing trip. *Christ provides.* The more, the merrier. He does it when nobody provides a place for him to lay his head, as he says. He shows us God's sort of love in his constant self-giving. God is a hospitable God. There is always room with him.

We need to remember that. We have plenty of chances to remember it when we trip over the discarded humanity all about us, bereft of the capacity to do much for themselves, cluttering up our doorways, sleeping in cardboard boxes for want of anyplace else to go — the ever-increasing homeless who settle for heating grates and subways. And not only those. Consider the people in your life who are alienated, who are kept from the door of your heart. You know whom I'm talking about. Only you know, and God. Your heart is not full. It has vacant spaces.

No room? Somehow we have to make room, because Christ cannot come to us when our hearts have empty spaces, but only when they are full of love for his beloved, whatever sort of people they may be. Then and only then can you add these two last lines of the mission hymn I quoted:

O come to my heart, Lord Jesus!
There is room in my heart for Thee.

Waiting for Us

You may remember a play from the sixties: Samuel Beckett's *Waiting for Godot*. Not much action in it, as I recall. Just a couple of street people sitting on a bench, chewing the fat. The fat was a parable, in its way. From the title you can guess that God, and waiting for him, was part of the message of the play.

Waiting for God. How can you wait to welcome someone you have never seen and who has never made a specific date and time for the meeting? The Bible tells us that "no one hath ever seen God at any time." How can you wait for some unimaginable presence? How can you know when the presence is with you? Unrecognized? Unrecognizable? And how will you know when the unrecognizable has withdrawn? Waiting for God is a frustrating exercise, if sitting around can be described as an exercise.

Frustrating not merely for us, but for God. For inherent in the whole business is the capacity for *mistake*. How can we know it's God? How can we know it *isn't* God — even if some think it might be God? And for God, there is the frustration of our failure to recognize him.

What about God waiting for us? Have you thought about that? Waiting for our recognition? Waiting for our welcome? Waiting for our greeting? Our acceptance? Our hospitality? With the track record of humanity, the chances are that he would be kept waiting forever before we would make a move to welcome him even if we recognized him. Curiously, however, this does not put him off. Despite the odds, the billion-to-one chance, he pockets his kingly, rightful pride, he divests himself of any claim to the blinding grandeur of his glory, he empties himself, as St. Paul says — *makes himself nothing* — and in silence, under the cover of night, in a God-forsaken corner of an inhospitable earth, he lies, waiting for us, as Robert Southwell (a young Elizabethan poet who died in 1591) says,

> . . . a simple tender babe,
> In freezing winter night
> In homely manger trembling lies
> Alas, a piteous sight.
> The inns are full; no man will yield
> This little pilgrim bed.
> But forced he is with simple beasts
> In crib to shroud his head.

Waiting for us, for our recognition, our welcome, our warmth, our *protection*, no less, helpless, powerless, hungry, and cold — that is how God comes to us, in contradiction of every possible notion, any stroke of the imagination. *Unimaginable.* Not in light, blinding light, but in the shadow of a cave on a December night. Not with trumpets, but with a baby's cry. Not in the flush of success or war and the enterprise of power but in the panic and the muddle of people being bullied into registering their family members for a Roman poll tax. When nerves were on edge, when resentment was running riot, when fear was the daily bread of the little people, God lay waiting among the little people — waiting for us all — and content to wait because of his name in prophecy, *Emmanuel,* "God with us." God with us in the din and gunfire thunder of Panama, in the frenzy and cruelty of Rumania, in the heady taste of freedom in the

21

Germanys, in the ill-contained impatience of Poland, in the breathless hope in Czechoslovakia, amid the rubble of concrete in San Francisco and the devastation on the islands, God with us under the roofs of the crack dens in Harlem and the seedy heroin hideouts in Colombia. Wherever there is devastation and horror, human debility and sin, there in the squalor and the muck lies a tiny child, waiting for us to take him in, waiting for us here and hereafter.

The Giver

The people who work in Bloomingdale's will tell you that Friday and Saturday will be days of stress this week. The store will be flooded by folks not satisfied with what they will be given tonight. They bring back the gifts for a frantic exchange for something else. This is one set of people who are not satisfied.

There is another set of people who are not satisfied. They are the givers of the unwanted gifts. There is a lot of hurt at rejection, much humiliation and frustration on the part of these givers. *They* are not satisfied. A Jewish friend of mine, Larry Wien, a philanthropist whose superb generosity has set him aside as one of New York's great givers (he provided the funds, unasked and out of the blue, for the outside of this church of St. Thomas to be cleaned this year) tells the story of this nice young Jewish man who was close to his mother and came to see her every Friday night. She sent him a birthday gift of two ties. The next Friday night when he came to her house, he wore one of the ties. When he came in, his mother said, "What's the matter, you don't like the other tie?" (from his "100 Stories").

This sermon is about the Giver — in this case, the Giver of All Gifts, as the ancient hymn describes God. If ever a giver were given cause to feel rejected, frustrated, humiliated, and maddened at the unconcern of the people he had given gifts to, it would be God. Look at what we take for granted and what we are never satisfied with: life itself, on this planet, cushioned by the genius of those who have given us the technologies that keep us warm, anesthetize pain, bring other worlds into our homes at the touch of a switch, bring loved ones to be with us from across the earth by plane or phone, protect us, sustain us, enthrall us with their music and their creativity. With pains beyond imagining and imagination excruciatingly detailed, he creates and provides a world fit for you and me to exist in *and to realize our potential in,* if we choose to do so and others allow us to do so. He takes the supreme risk in all this of bestowing upon humanity the freedom he himself enjoys, so that we are absolutely free to accept what we are given, be pleased with what we are given, use what we are given with the love he has implanted within us from his own heart of love, create from what we are given with that creative energy of his which he imparts to all his children — or be absolutely free to turn up our noses and turn our backs upon the gifts of the Giver. Which is pretty much what we have done. You would think that our rejected and humiliated Creator might seek vengeance. He does.

There is all the difference in the world between human and divine vengeance. Ours is tainted with a hunger for an eye for an eye and a tooth for a tooth. If we can add something more severe for good measure, chances are that we will. The divine vengeance is different. God's mercy *is* his vengeance. Don't ask me how, but that is what happens, and people who have loved God and made a life study of his ways will all tell you that.

Supremely do we see it at this time. The world has always been preoccupied with itself — loving itself, hating itself, vaunting itself, exploiting itself, with scarcely a thought for the heart of love that makes the world go round, hardly a remembrance of the generosity of the Giver and

Sustainer of life and the Source of all our wisdom and inventiveness. It has found itself fascinating, and it is in one hell of a mess. Just that. One *hell* of a mess — a mess and a predicament without God, which is what hell can in the end mean.

God gets his own back at our selfish self-*in*sufficiency by bringing his vengeance not in a cataclysm, not in a calamity, but in a baby's cry. He himself suddenly is among us as we are, one of us, helpless and vulnerable like the least of us, poor like most of us, dependent on love like all of us. He places himself in our predicament, he gives himself to a world that has never dreamt he would do it and has never really wanted him among us. That is his vengeance. His vengeance is his mercy. He simply would not take No for an answer, and risked being unwanted, unrecognized, unwelcome, and generally in the way. If we will not give ourselves in love to him, his vengeance has been that he will give himself to us. To do it, he courts disaster. To do it, he invites disagreement. He takes that risk. He comes, and he appears in a situation that is unfortunate, ill-timed so far as the world's inconvenience and comfort are concerned. We would put him off forever if we could. He becomes the uninvited guest, he becomes the man who came to dinner and brought not respectability to the table, not good luck or even conviviality, but food — food for life eternal. Himself. He keeps on bringing himself to our table of discontent and disappointment, failure and foolishness. He sweetens our diet and keeps us alive.

The secret is that his vengeance has succeeded. He has won. He has reclaimed us for himself, us whom he loves and gives life to. True it is then, in every meaning of the phrase, that God the Giver *has got his own back.*

Utterly Irrelevant?

It is a sad fact in our lives that certain folks and certain faces and certain names and certain actions never fit, are always out of place, incongruous, perhaps embarrassing. They confront us suddenly. They are there and we are here, and we don't know how or why they got there. They are impossible to ignore and they stop us in our tracks. Do you remember this protest song from one of the shows in the fifties?

> In the summer, you're the winter;
> In the finger, you're the splinter;
> In the banquet, you're the stew —
> Say! I can do without you!

These incongruities are puzzling, sometimes fascinating.

Just after the Trump Tower was opened, I passed and looked at the imposing soldier-figure guarding the doors on Fifth Avenue. There he was in his big black bearskin helmet, his scarlet guardsman's dress uniform tunic like a grenadier. And on his feet: Guccis.

The supreme incongruity is why we are here tonight. If ever an event flew in the face of the expected, the reasonable, the acceptable, this was it. For at the worst possible time for a family harassed and homeless on its way to be registered, the baby started to arrive. In surroundings desolate and inhospitable, God chose to make his appearance —

the very opposite of anything that could be termed *desirable*. That tiny child *was* the supreme incongruity in a world unready, unable to cope, at odds with itself, at the mercy of the greedy and the ambitious, paralyzed by terror and petrified by fear and superstition. God could have done much better, but he chose not to grace the occasion with some superlative show. He came in secrecy, under cover of night rather than the light of a blazing sun, and settled among muddle and resentment and dingy poverty. And he has stayed there ever since. True it is, he fills the earth. But assuredly he is to be found among people at the end of their tether, the unsuccessful, the defeated, the disappointed, and the bereft, those for whom life has disintegrated, and those battered beyond hope by circumstances of poverty, political oppression, personal inadequacy, or intellectual insufficiency — the people we talk about when we parody Christ's words about the poor being always with us.

And because he is here, that little Bethlehem baby will always be unsuitable to the powerful and the violent in the heat of their rages, the crucible of their hatreds. In the summer of their discontent, he will be the winter, confronting them with the coolness of meek obedience and the icy courage of the obedience of which the Scriptures speak — "that obedience unto death, even the death of the cross. Wherefore God hath highly exalted him and given him a name which is above every other name: that at the name of Jesus every knee shall bow and every tongue confess that Jesus Christ is Lord to the glory of God the Father."

And because he is with us, that little Bethlehem baby will always be a nuisance to the ambitious and the greedy who finagle for their own advantage and whose fingers itch for personal success at the expense of lesser souls. That self-giving love will always be the splinter in those fingers; it will always mar their efficiency at getting and holding. Somehow the tight grasp of dishonest success will have a

27

twinge that will spoil its enjoyment. When self-giving love gets in the way of the ruthless grab, the triumph is thwarted somehow. Christ does it all the time because he knows from the pain in his own hands the tale the nails can tell, as he touches in blessing those who come to him in love.

And because he is with us, he will always be an embarrassment to the complacent, he will be the stew in the banquet of their conceit, their hardness of heart, and their contempt for God's Word and commandments. He will always be out of place, always irrelevant in lives that have only time for themselves. But he will never cease loving them and shyly trying to get them to taste his stew, for if they do so, as Scripture points out, they will "taste and see how gracious the Lord is."

And because he is here with us, he will always be the clown, the ridiculous one with the wrong shoes among those who take themselves seriously, the superior, the proud, the self-conscious, and the cruel. He will always, so to speak, be the guardsman with the Guccis, "despised, rejected of men, a man of sorrows, and acquainted with grief," the one people laugh at as he hangs on his cross, the one whom people never take seriously. It requires the innocence of a child to understand what he is really up to, and he tells us that without such childlike innocence, without being born again, we will continue to miss the point to our own ruination and sorrow.

> In the summer, you're the winter;
> In the finger, you're the splinter;
> In the banquet, you're the stew —
> Say! I can do without you!

Of course we can do without him, but he has no intention that we shall if he can help it. He has come tonight. He has come here tonight. And he is here to stay. That's what his name means: Emmanuel, God with us. And he is looking to you for a welcome, a hand, an embrace, waiting for you to say,

> O come to my heart, Lord Jesus!
> There is room in my heart for Thee.

God's Hidden Agenda

It is just conceivable that some of you are old enough to remember the Broadway musical *Guys and Dolls*. There is a song in it that begins

> Take back your mink
> Take back your pearls
> What makes you think
> That I was one of those girls?

The young lady is outraged to discover that her admirer has a *hidden agenda,* in this case something more than the friendship he has asked for, more than the evidences of regard he has provided in the mink and pearls.

A hidden agenda is something we usually dislike when we discover it. For while one thing is being discussed, there are other things on the mind of more pressing importance, and they are the real issue.

Forever at this season we need to remember that there is such a thing as a divine hidden agenda. God has a hidden agenda, and it is all for our present blessedness and future joy, for what God has in mind is above what we can desire or deserve, realms away from what we can imagine.

True, he says things we *think* we understand. We don't always like what he tells us, for his word is not what we want to hear, not what we hasten to recognize, not what we wish to apply to ourselves. It is the word of judgment, and we do not like judgment. We resent being "weighed in the balance and found wanting," as the Scriptures say. It is the word of holiness, and that is a rebuke to our selfish ways and our pride, our dearest possession, what we are the most reluctant of all to become poor in. It is the word of self-negation and heavy cross-carrying and going the extra mile and giving away things and forgiving eternally. His word is, as the writer of the Epistle to the Hebrews says, alive and active. It cuts more keenly than any two-edged sword, piercing as far as the place where life and spirit, joints and marrow divide. It sifts the thoughts and purposes of the heart (Heb. 4:12).

If that is what he is discussing, then it is more comfortable not to have to listen, and easier not to have to obey.

But God has a hidden agenda. It is not some selfish plan but a desire for us to climb the ladder of hope and find peace in believing. What God has in mind is that you should have Somebody to turn to, to rely upon, to be comforted by, to be inspired by and motivated by, to be strengthened for the inevitable struggles between your worse self and your better self. Yes, he comes to us where we are. That is the story of Christmas . . . how he made us to enjoy life as he enjoys life — only by giving ourselves willingly and voluntarily to him in love. And when we withheld that love and kept it to rot in the love for ourselves, he thwarted our pride and gave himself to us in an irrevocable and irreversible act of unselfishness, and he did it in a stupendous way, in a cave, through an unknown girl, on some hidden night.

He comes to us where we are, and he accepts us — but not as we are. That is the figment of our selfish imaginations. He has other ideas. He has a hidden agenda. Listen to St. John again:

> He came unto his own, and his own received him not. But as many as received him, to them gave he power to become the

31

sons of God, even to them that believe on his name: Which were born, not of blood, nor of the will of the flesh, nor of the will of man, but of God.

John 1:11-13, KJV

That is his hidden agenda. Power is the name of the divine game, but not necessarily the power we know, not the power we want, not the power we admire. *Power to become the sons of God* is of a different sort. It has to do with liberty, with the ability to love God. It is the freedom to love unashamedly, honestly, and unselfishly, "not for the sake of gaining aught, or seeking a reward."

It is the inner authority that folks are given when they have integrity, when they are "together," which is what *integrity* means. When they can see straight, think straight, love strongly, discern needs and lacks and longing. When they are *tender:* when they "rejoice with those who rejoice and weep with them that weep," as the Scriptures say. And they can do this because there is an inner certainty of a mysterious power of love somewhere beyond them that yet encompasses them, embraces them, holds them fast, and makes them better. We call it *redeeming love.*

That is the power. It takes you onward, out of yourself. It makes you better. Not that you will be conscious of feeling better about yourself — that is transient, and it can be narcissistic. Not that you will be conscious of strength. You are conscious instead of desire — the desire to love Christ first, to open your heart to share its desire for generosity, to be forgiving, to be filled with a thirst for justice and a passionate resolve to be of help because you see him in the eyes of the people who surround you. And this, my friends, is what the Bible calls "the glorious liberty of the children of God."

And it is yours for the asking, this authority, this power — yours when you find room in the inn of your heart for this child, who hides behind the eyes of God's children everywhere who need our love and our welcome, our acceptance and a share in our joy.

> Where children pure and happy
> pray to the blessed Child.
> Where misery cries out to Thee
> Son of the mother mild.
> Where charity stands watching
> and faith holds wide the door,
> The dark night wakes, the glory breaks
> And Christmas comes once more.

An Inappropriate Present

Some of you who were around last year may remember my observing Father Fertig, the bearded and genial vicar of this place, constantly leaving the parish house laden with shopping bags full of Christmas gifts from grateful parishioners. When I could bear it no longer, I said, "It's obvious that the parishioners respect the rector. They *love* the curates!" Never having been able to leave well enough alone, I got back to the subject this past week when I saw his office sofa groaning with parcels and packages. "Yes," he replied, "if you were nicer, you'd get presents."

The story of this holy night is the story of a gift. Not to nice people. Not to discerning or deserving people. Not to people hoping to be remembered. Not to people ready to receive anything at all. The gift was given to a nasty world of spoiled people who wanted a lot but had no sense of what they really needed. The gift was utterly out of place, inappropriate in the judgment of the wise, and what was worse, the worst of all, a liability.

The situation looked like this. What do you do with a human race unsure of its own capacity to answer all the questions and to cope with many answers? Proud empires had arisen. Great discoveries had been made. There was plenty of beauty and plenty of talent. There was a lot of truth in that beauty, too. But there was fear and there was torment. Superstition hung like a cloud over the nations, distorting their hopes, their sense of destiny. Cruelty ran riot. In the midst of all this, the idea of a loving and faithful Creator was shared by a tiny few who clung to the things their prophets and wise people had spoken. But they were despised and unsuccessful in the world game of power and domination. They treasured these promises, pathetic and irrational as they seemed to the successful, the powerful, the victorious, and the arrogant. What on earth could it ever matter that

> A virgin shall conceive
> and bear a son
> and they shall call his name Emmanuel . . . ?

> Unto us a son is given: and the government shall be upon his shoulder: and his name shall be called

>> Wonderful,
>> Counsellor,
>> The mighty God,
>> The everlasting Father,
>> The Prince of Peace.

> Of the increase of his government and peace there shall be no end, upon the throne of David, and upon his kingdom, to order it, and to establish it with judgment and with justice from henceforth even for ever.

> Isaiah 9:6-7, KJV

What could it matter, when there was no earthly possibility of political or military power for this puny and pettifogging nation with its dietary laws and its preoccupation with its divine destiny?

There is always in God's dealing with us an element of the *inappropriate*. In his humility he never looks to see if his shirttail has been tucked in or if we are ready and our faces arranged to give him a polite acknowledgment. He

35

simply comes to us in silence and hands us himself in his Son, and then just as suddenly disappears from sight, leaving us holding the baby, in every sense of the term. The last thing we want around is yet another *dependent*. And God has never paused to allow us to be nice to him or to place ourselves in the position of deserving what he may choose to bestow upon us. We stare at what we have been given, aghast at what we are now liable for with this gift, wondering how we can relate to him. The poor seem better able to understand him than the sophisticated, for the poor are more familiar with having another mouth to feed, used to making do. Somehow he has to be accommodated. Somehow he has to be told he is welcome. For he is here and he is here to stay. God *with* us — that is what the name *Emmanuel* means. And he will live to turn many of our attitudes and presuppositions upside down. He will discountenance us because, although having nothing, he nonetheless has a generosity that will stagger us, an understanding that will mystify us, a peace that will flatten us, a love that will wash over us and make us clean and give us hope and transfer to the dim candles of our faith light enough to see by. And then we notice a strange family likeness in him and in the faces of those who have decided to give him house room, for he has a capacity to make himself at home.

> How silently, how silently,
>   the wondrous gift is giv'n!
> So God imparts to human hearts
>   the blessings of his heav'n.
> No ear may hear his coming,
>   but in this world of sin,
> Where meek souls will receive him,
>   still the dear Christ enters in.

On Not Shutting the Door

"The trouble with American hospitality is not how to return it, but how to survive it." Prince Philip said that in my hearing in this city over thirty years ago. It is true. One of the characteristic features and noble attributes of the American people is seen in their favorite national celebration, Thanksgiving — not the commemoration of a victory in battle or the storming of some vile prison but a remembrance of a meal shared in 1621 in deep gratitude to God for survival. Hospitality lies deep in the heart here, and it stems from gratitude to God.

St. John, in the prologue to his Gospel, one of the most glorious pieces of prose ever written, has this subject at the back of his mind when he writes this chilling phrase about what happened to Christ, the Word of God: "He came unto his own, and his own received him not" (John 1:11, KJV). In one bleak phrase he describes a lack of hospitality. It could be that Christ's own folk, his country and nation, were unaware of who he was and what he was about. It could be that they didn't want to know. But, for whatever reason, "he came unto his own, and his own received him not." There was no welcome. No door was open for him. It began as he was about to be born. No room at the inn. No hand to beckon him inside. He was made to feel that he did not belong, that he had nothing of interest or value for them. The doors were shut. "They received him not."

Fear can do this. A terrible, self-protective selfishness is the child of fear. You know as well as I do that we aren't always ready to receive and accept, for fear that we may be obligated, compromised, somehow put at a disadvantage. Whether it's an offer of a gift of love, which may make us uncomfortable because we are no longer in control of the situation when someone else takes the initiative, or whether the gift is so large as to be embarrassing, or whether as men it offends our stupid sense of masculinity and machismo to have to receive instead of to give, the fact is that pride can spoil the act of receiving. We view gifts not as opportunities but as unwelcome intrusions into our way of doing things, and so we decline many offers. And when we are called to accept people with problems, like the homeless who shiver on our streets, and we respond by slamming the doors to our hearts, that is an added sign of an ugly fear.

Weren't you saddened by the neighborhood's violent and angry rejection of the proposal that an unused Roman Catholic parish building be used to house sufferers from AIDS? Whatever the motive for these protests might be, it drives home the point that wherever the human heart beats there is the capacity for saying "No room!" Put it down to prejudice. Put it down to fear. Put it down to pride. It is all the same evil blossom from the same root of that stinkweed, human sin. And I have a suspicion that on the first Christmas it was this precise predicament, human self-preoccupation, that God wished to redeem and cure by subjecting himself in his Son to it, in the very area where people make the most of it: *their money.*

Do you remember the clue to this suspicion I have? "There went out a decree from Caesar Augustus that all the world should be taxed." The Roman emperor wanted the name and address of everybody who lived within the monstrous empire enjoying the Pax Romana, the Roman Peace. This wasn't a survey for scientific or sociological purposes. This was for *money* — money to pay for the maintenance of the Roman Peace. And that meant armies, and roads the armies could march along, and walls to keep enemies out, and wages and food to keep the armies in, and ships and weapons and fortresses and officials and residences. It had to come from somewhere, from somebody. Those people happened to be there, however unwillingly. The money was to come from them. Mention taxes and people get very nasty — with the government, with each other, even with themselves. It was at the moment of multinational insecurity and misery and fear and apprehension at forthcoming loss, loss of a thing that distinguished them from their neighbors — money — that Christ suddenly appeared.

They weren't Christmas crowds buying presents and wondering what to give and hoping what to get. They were worried and resentful hordes having their privacy invaded. There was precious little space for welcome or hospitality in this preoccupied time. We can understand that! But we must realize that *how* we react is very revealing in situations where our generosity and hospitality is sought without warning. History, on the whole, has a sorry tale to tell. And even a nation with as great a reputation for hospitality as ours has to beware of resting on its laurels. Mayor Koch could tell us that. We have heard him plead for acceptance of many groups of inconvenient people and institutions.

But John doesn't end there. "But as many as received him, to them gave he power to become the sons of God" (John 1:12, KJV) — that is, the privilege of belonging to Christ as his brother.

This is the night of the year, this holy night, when he comes to his own for recognition and for welcome. He hopes to find you at home to him, hospitable to him, open to him as you recognize him for who he is, open to him in the people who come to us for help and whom he calls his brothers and sisters, because he wants to be in you, to live in you for others, that the doors to them may never be shut: Emmanuel, God here with us, and here to stay, recognized, welcomed, warmed by us as we say of him:

> The fount of Mary's joy
>   Revealed now lies,
> For, lo, has not the Boy
>   His Father's eyes?

Charles L. O'Donnell

The Irony of It All

Have you noticed that there is a certain irony in the message this holy night brings, the message of peace on the earth to people of goodwill? The coming of Christmas after its heralded and hectic approach falls like a gentle blanket upon our streets and airports and covers the land with a silence that we notice because we're not used to it. Have you for instance ever found yourself at J.F.K. on a late Christmas afternoon? The place echoes with emptiness. People are at home, inside, with their families and their friends, probably eating or letting sleep help them recover from it. The streets are deserted. It is an extraordinary testimony to the power of the life of a baby in Bethlehem some two thousand years ago that the whole world seems to take a deep breath, hold its peace, and allow a tiny child to take center stage as his birth is remembered, re-enacted, portrayed, and fondly sung. Church bells break the silence of this time as they bring the news again to a waiting earth. All for a baby!

The irony of it is that this holy celebration is taken advantage of. Businesses make fortunes, and individuals part with fortunes as they buy what the business world makes — to celebrate Christmas. People find that they give what they can't afford to buy, presents that the recipients frequently don't like. It is a strange time of commerce and exchange. You can tell from people's faces on Fifth Avenue, from their glazed and preoccupied looks, that they are behind with their schedules, that the choice for their mother-in-law's gift for some reason eludes them, and desperation stares them in the face. That is the other side, the ironic side, of Christmas.

And then, consider what the world has been up to before the deep breath that it seems to take as it holds its peace briefly to allow this tiny child to take center stage. I'm not sure if ever amid the eighteen Christmases I have spent here with you there has been such a hurricane of events thundering and screaming around the planet. Europe is in convulsion as nations choose freedom and struggle for it, turning one country after another inside out and upside down. First Poland, then states in Soviet Russia, then East Germany, then Hungary, then Czechoslovakia, then Bulgaria, now Rumania. The landscape is unrecognizable compared to this time last year. In all this turmoil, above the thunder of nations, the shouts of triumph as walls of separation come crashing down and people flood through the Brandenburg Gates of countries long shackled — above it all, there is the cry of a newborn child, and souls know that Emmanuel, God with us, is here. Here, and here to stay.

> For unto us a child is born, unto us a son is given: and the government shall be upon his shoulder: and his name shall be called
>
> Wonderful,
> Counsellor,
> The Mighty God,
> The Everlasting Father,
> The Prince of Peace.
>
> Of the increase of his government and peace there shall be no end.
>
> Isaiah 9:6-7a, KJV

And I profoundly believe — I am persuaded, as St. Paul would say — that this prophecy will prove itself true in its entirety, though I have no way to guess when. I am equally convinced that the prophet of old was aware of the potential irony of it all — the ridiculousness of the whole concept, because he was no stranger to the forces and events of his day of which today's cataclysms in Europe are a later reflection. In his day empires rose and stood in cruelty and power and fell away in pieces like our Berlin Wall. In his day dangerous men sought to control nations and were put down like Ceaucescu of Rumania — run out of the place by angry people who had suffered enough. In his day, the inequity of wealth and the hunger of the poor were as common as they are to us. But through all this he spoke of his certainty that the divine victory would emerge and God's peaceful rule would be established — with the birth of a child, with all the vulnerability and the helplessness of an infant, and not through violent conquest. The irony of it all, the upside-downness of it all, the impossibility, the implausibility of it all, is writ large in the story of God's people, and we gather to celebrate it tonight.

Earlier at Lessons and Carols I mentioned an Elizabethan poet, Robert Southwell, who died young, in his thirties, in 1591. He gave evidence of an extraordinary gift of understanding this irony in poems he wrote about the birth of Christ, poems later taken by Benjamin Britten and set to music in his magnificently lovely "Ceremony of Carols."

Listen. The boy choristers will know these words by heart:

> This little Babe so few days old,
> Is come to rifle Satan's fold;
> All hell doth at his presence quake,
> Though he himself for cold do shake;
> For in this weak unarmed wise
> The gates of hell he will surprise.

43

With tears he fights and wins the field,
His naked breast stands for a shield;
His battering shot are babish cries,
His arrows looks of weeping eyes,
His martial ensigns Cold and Need,
And feeble Flesh his warrior's steed.

His camp is pitched in a stall,
His bulwark but a broken wall;
The crib his trench, haystalks his stakes;
Of shepherds he his muster makes;
And thus, as sure his foe to wound,
The angels' trumps alarum sound.

My soul, with Christ join thou in fight;
Stick to the tents that he hath pight.
Within his crib is surest ward;
This little Babe will be thy guard.
If thou wilt foil thy foes with joy,
Then flit not from this heavenly Boy.

Good News as Bad News

Anybody who works around here will tell you that at the times of the Christian year when we get ready to rejoice, such as at Christmas or Easter, when we are preparing in heart and mind to be happy, the devil gets very busily to work to disrupt and destroy, to dismay and disappoint the delight of the people of God. You may have heard me say before that I myself have never caught a glimpse of that forked tail, but I have occasionally caught a whiff of sulphur . . .

It is a low point in the year for whatever it is that is at enmity with God. It is a point of desperation for all that is evil at the prospect of the light and warmth of the truth of Christmas or Easter making themselves felt not merely to believers but to anybody whose heart is not made of brick. We can attest that there have been conversions to Christ in this very place around Christmas and Easter, when the Christ presence mysteriously became a reality to a heart ready for the reality to happen without perhaps realizing it. Do you wonder then that the devil gets going, that there seems, from some mysterious and unexpected spring of evil and wrong-mindedness, to spew a well of bitter-tasting water and a spirit of destructiveness? It is not necessarily serious. It is never catastrophic. But it happens. Good people get tired, and their resistance is low — resistance to their lesser selves, resistance to the temptation to impatience. Small hitches assume the stature of disaster. Tempers can become uncertain as the "devil walketh about, seeking whom he may devour." When resistance is low, it becomes difficult "to resist, steadfast in the faith." We have noticed this.

But it is nothing new. It is a symptom of an age-old phenomenon of goodness finally openly declaring itself, of holiness taking flesh and expressing itself through a human life. For, you see, godliness, holiness, divine goodness, is true reality. God is supreme reality in himself, and all that is not of him is that much less real, for being that much less true to him and to itself. And the disturbing thing is that reality is too much for some people. The Scriptures report this when St. John in his Gospel records Jesus as saying, "the light has come into the world, but men preferred darkness to light" (3:19, NEB).

Such a man was Herod. It is his reaction that sets a background of darkness to the Epiphany story. The word *epiphany* means a breakthrough of light, like a beam from a lighthouse piercing fog and dark mist. The light of God suddenly and unexpectedly appears and shows itself, in the form of a star, to some astrologers who follow its path to the country where old Herod sits on his shaky throne. They confront him with the news, and the light of a new reality hits his eyes.

What would you say if a total stranger with access to information unknown to you told you that your property and possessions would become somebody else's, totally unconnected with yourself or your family? It must have been an extraordinarily awkward interview: three stargazers, from God knows where, telling this piece of news to old King Herod the Great. He had been the puppet king since 40 B.C., when the Romans had put him there. He had sired an heir and held on to what he had been given for nearly thirty-seven years through a mixture of efficiency and ruthlessness combined with diplomacy. Then in walked three astrologers who, like some academics, displayed more enthusiasm for their subject than tact — the sort of people who either bore you or scare you. They told the king of the Jews with an established heir that they had come seeking a child who was born to be king of the Jews so they could pay him homage. They had seen his star — *his* star, in the ascendant. They followed where it led them, from the East. And it had stopped. There. It's the ancient and classic example of the "good news/bad news" story.

Reality, when one is confronted with it, can be an unpleasant jolt. It can be too much for some people. Some of you will remember the play in which Ralph Richardson took the part of an inadequate man with an impossible dream, to possess an apple orchard. To acquire it, he cheated and stole from his wife even when it was still a figment of his imagination. It so happened that he came into the possession of an orchard, but when he did, the reality was too much for him. Some people cannot cope with reality. It paralyzes them or reduces them or leads them to violence or self-destruction.

Reality came to King Herod in the innocent tactlessness of fortune tellers. "When Herod the king had heard these things, he was troubled, and all Jerusalem with him." For all Jerusalem somehow overheard. The courtiers leaked it. A wall of security was broken, and the flimsy security of King Herod and his kingdom was shattered. A new king? A supplanter king? A new Jacob (his name meant "supplanter")? Not if Herod could help it. Reality made him violent. He ordered death for male children of two and under in the little towns and villages surrounding Bethlehem. The stargazers' naivete brought death to innocents at the hands of a disturbed and desperate ruler. We must remember that. It was not their fault. It was a terrible concomitant to their visit.

Reality can be too much for some. Think of a political reality that is tearing a country in the Middle East apart. There, within the borders of Israel, sit hundreds of thousands of Arabs. The fact is that hell will freeze over before those Arabs stop hoping that the parcel of land that contains them on the West Bank will one day be entirely and wholly theirs again. That is one political reality. The other political reality is that the land is occupied territory — occupied by Israel, which has no intention of fulfilling the Arab dream. The third political reality is that both sides are resorting to physical violence — the Arabs from frustration, the Jews from desperation. *The realities are too much* for them both. Hatred, contempt, and a desire for revenge have caused overreactions and deplorably cruel retaliations by the Israeli troops. That is another form of reality. Will no one calm down long enough to stop a conflagration? There is evil in this hatred. There is evil in this violence. There is evil in this revenge. The realities are too much for both.

Some people cannot cope with the reality of love and commitment. They simply cannot cope with it. They are incapable of sustaining a relationship unless it is on their own terms. Parity puzzles them, frightens them, and they seek to escape the legitimate responsibilities that strong love brings with it. Some people cannot cope with the reality of another loving somebody else, not themselves. And some people are less able to cope with the reality of success than of failure. Success spoils some people, making their perspective lopsided and their priorities self-centered. We have seen how the power associated with success can corrupt, how absolute power can corrupt absolutely. We are familiar with these things. We've seen it on Wall Street. We've seen it in Washington. We've seen it around the mayor's colleagues in this city.

I have seen reality overwhelm friends in the priesthood. Not the reality of success, nor necessarily the reality of love,

but the reality of living with the consequences of their actions. I knew Gary Bennett, the priest who committed suicide
in Oxford just before Christmas. . . . I knew his dismay at
what he thought the Church had sunk to. I knew of his long
friendship with the Archbishop. What I did not know but
what I can imagine is his horror at what happened when
his preface was published and the press seized upon two or
three sentences referring to the Archbishop and called it an
attack. It was too much for Fr. Bennett. And we know what
happened to him.

But reality is meant to strengthen us. The Holy Spirit
of Truth is the Strengthener, the Comforter, the Encourager,
and the Friend at our side, Christ in us, living on in us. We
know that St. John in all the experience of his soul's contemplation of this mystery was quite clear about it all, and
that is what this Sunday's worship is all about: "The light
shines in the darkness, and the darkness has *never* quenched
it."

There, under Your Nose — All the Time

I think I have made an important biological discovery. People's arms, I notice, get shorter in their middle forties. I discovered this ten years ago when I reached for a Manhattan telephone directory and couldn't read the print one morning. I held the thing further away. Then further, until I realized that not only was my hair thinning but my reach had shortened. I don't know why it happens like that. But I would warn the vicar that it could happen to him sooner than he might realize, sooner than his beard can whiten.

So things under one's nose don't easily make themselves seen, and details blur. The things are there, to be sure, but they elude our notice until certain perspectives are achieved. When that happens, we can see the forest despite the trees. Before that happens, we often cannot.

So it is with God and ourselves. Always and everywhere available to us, breathing life into our life, sustaining us and all things, the source of all our logic as well as our life, God waits. Do you remember that remarkable account in the Old Testament, of the prophet Elijah, who wondered where God could be.

> And he said, Go forth, and stand upon the mount before the LORD. And, behold, the LORD passed by, and a great and strong wind rent the mountains, and brake in pieces the rocks before the LORD; but the LORD was not in the wind: and after

the wind an earthquake; but the LORD was not in the earthquake: And after the earthquake a fire; but the LORD was not
in the fire: and after the fire a still small voice.

1 Kings 19:11-12, KJV

It was there, all the time, and yet that still, small voice
went unheard, unnoticed, despite its persistency. All you
have to do is talk loud or talk big, and you will never hear
that voice. Since we spend most of our waking lives talking
loud or talking big or doing both at the same time, endlessly
fascinated with the endless monologue about ourselves, we
stand a good chance of *never* being able to catch that sound.
The earthquake of events that make us unsteady and unsure
on our feet and the whirlwind of lives constantly spinning
around us and making such a noise doing it don't allow
much notice of the God who waits. To hear the still, small
voice, you have to listen. That means concentration, and
silence, and a certain amount of quiescence. For a get-up-
and-go civilization like ours, *that* sort of medicine puts one
in mind of the motto Listerine used to have: "The taste
people hate." But it might do us a power of good.

When Christ came among us, here, and here to stay, it
was only by a fluke, the merest chance, that people noticed
that he was here at all. A star is a chancy thing. You have
to be a stargazer to hope to notice it. And the weather has
to favor you. Just one cloud in the wrong place, and the
chances diminish to nothing. The star that attracted the
attention of that group of astrologers and magicians was
one of millions: it was a million-to-one chance that they saw
it at all. But they did, because God was waiting to make
himself known. They were prepared to look and wait and
consider. Their chance discovery was in reality no chance at
all, no coincidence. Silently and shyly, God waits to make
himself known. The tiny light is seen for what it is.

Meanwhile, back at the ranch, so to speak, in

Jerusalem, where King Herod sits fidgeting in fear of being edged out of power, he has earthquakes of his own to contend with. He does not stand firm in his possession of the throne. He is there only because he has given a guarantee to the Romans that he can keep the peace, and he has had to murder potential rivals to do it. He is on shaky territory, trusted by neither his masters nor his subjects, and insurrection and rebellion are never far from his mind. Or theirs. If you were in that position yourself, how would you feel about a bunch of enthusiastic astrologers who came to your troubled house bringing news of the appearance of some unsuspected king? "When Herod the king heard this, he was troubled, and all Jerusalem with him" (Matt. 2:3, RSV). All Jerusalem, too? People talk. Have you noticed? The whirlwind of rumor and embellishment had begun, fueled by political speculations and a preoccupation with all the possibilities and remedies and strategies that suspicion can create. The place was a vortex of gales of arguments and apprehensions about rival monarchies and power grabbing. Small wonder that the whole lot missed hearing the sound of God. The defenseless truth eluded them all, for nobody stopped to think that the still, small voice of a baby could be the sound of God making his home among us. Until too late. Too late! He is here, and here to stay.

And so there has to be a search, a rooting out, an elimination, and Herod murders babies just as Pharaoh had in the Egypt of Israel's history. The earthquake does not stop, the whirlwind of anxiety continues to howl, for no one can be sure, and a nation chosen by the Lord cannot hear what it would so love to hear: the voice of its God.

But the eccentric astrologers hear it, and they gaze upon the source of all glory — the God who made the heavens. And they *worship* a child in his simplicity.

This throws me back, for I have to learn a new alphabet. The one I had learned tells all about the human search for self-identity, the importance of taking initiative with integrity in order to discover the important things about life and about myself. All that is right, as far as it goes. But there is another alphabet to learn, and it starts from the "Z" end. The end is really the beginning for me, because God, my end, is already here and waiting as he speaks in his still, small voice, waiting for me to distinguish it, to recognize it, to welcome it, and to "give back the song . . . which now the angels sing." "In the end is my beginning," and the truth of it comes clearer today as we celebrate the Epiphany, the showing forth of God, the Son of God, for he is here, and has been here an eternity, waiting for me to be found by him.

It is a warning to the church. How often have we heard that the church is shortsighted, that she plans poorly, that her strategy is archaic, that her teaching is simply irrelevant and out of date, and that she can see no further than the end of her nose? But what about the possibility of her being farsighted, striving after grandiose ends without being careful and watchful concerning the means to those ends. Does she overlook the things she should be attending to because they are too near to see clearly, as when in her desire to be the first in the world to consecrate a woman as bishop, she provided the Church in America with an embarrassment, choosing a divorcee without any seminary training when among the women priests there are magnificent examples of leadership and sound learning and deep godliness? We have an appalling situation on our hands. Or in the case of schemes to desex the language in sacred Scripture and liturgy, do people forget Christ's claim to be the Son of the heavenly Father in their eagerness for an earthly equality? Or do those training your clergy neglect the knowledge and love of the Word of God and its proclamation in favor of expertise in psychological methods for dealing with individuals? Are we concentrating on the horizontal to the point of neglecting the vertical, the eternal dimension?

Our Lord knows only too well this snare of farsightedness. Make sure, he says, to take the time to ensure that your foundations are sound before you proceed with a big building project. He gives the Pharisees something uncomfortable to think about when he accuses them, for all their moral grandeur and spiritual superiority, of being "inwardly . . . ravening wolves" (Matt. 7:15, KJV). The kingdom of God, he says, is a vast tree, and the nesting home of birds, but it begins as a tiny seed, carefully planted. These particular truths are part of himself, and like himself, they have been here all the time, unnoticed by the self-preoccupied, unexpected by the busy and the beleaguered. But to those *with ears to hear,* as he says, that still, small voice of him in his truth will make itself heard, and he will show himself in it.

And if you wonder why God seems to prefer this way of disclosing himself, might it not be because he has no wish to terrify us into recognition of him or to impress us into appreciation of him, but rather chooses to show us by humility and gentleness that he waits until we are found by him to make himself known and recognized and loved and answered in the tone of his voice?

Getting to the Nitty-Gritty

We are now in the countdown to Lent. Within three days we shall be facing the necessity for making choices, some of them painful. Painful, I said: not melancholy. We don't heave a sad sigh as our dietary regimes take a plainer turning; we don't cast a last longing gloomy glance at the vodka bottle. Pain isn't alien to joy. Who says so? I'll tell you who says so. The author of the letter to the Hebrews says so, of Christ himself, "who for the joy that was before him endured the cross, despising the shame, and is seated at the right hand of the throne of God" (Heb. 12:2, RSV). For the joy that was before him, awaiting him, and *with* him at one and the same time, in the way that so many mysterious paradoxes find their resolution in him, he faced the pain and the dereliction and the desertion and the indignities of his passion. He took up his cross gladly, and he tells us that he expects us to do the same with ours. Lent is the time realistically and without sentimentality to consider the implications of cross-carrying, for love of him, that his joy may be in us, and that our joy may be full, as he promises.

Lent is all for joy. So Lent loses what it never should have had in the first place, that February wet dreariness, in its anticipation of the "glory which is to be revealed" in the joy of Christ. That glory, that splendor, we are told by Paul in the lesson we heard today from his letter to the Christians in Corinth, is our privilege and our heritage, those of us who own the faith of Jesus. Paul says "we all reflect as in a mirror the splendour of the Lord; thus we are transfigured into his likeness, from splendour to splendour" (2 Cor. 3:18, NEB). When Christ tells us to let our light so shine before men that they can see our good works and give glory to our Father who is in heaven, he is only saying that in seeing the reflection of his likeness the people of the world will be drawn to the love that is in him and find themselves giving God the Father the praise and glory for the joy they discover in beholding his glory.

That, my friends, is the theological setting for Lent. It is all for joy. It is all for Christ. And what we take on, we take on gladly as the cross he expects us to shoulder for love of him.

It is as simple and as profound and as painful and as costly and as marvelous as that.

Grasp that, and the practicalities become clear: no longer a nuisance, no longer a drag, no longer long faces. Christ will have none of that, and he tells us so. Plainly.

Some of you may have read what I wrote in a letter I sent to the parish about Lent and its observance. I want to quote from it because I can't express better what I want to say.

> The more I think about it, the more I am certain that our observance of Lent should hit hard where it hurts most, wherever that place in our lives and in our preferences finds itself. It goes without saying that to deny yourself accustomed luxuries in Lent is something that has to be done seriously, which may mean that the expenditure of money may be involved, in which case the money should be given to a worthy cause. Make no bones about this, and be strict with yourself over fudging the issue.

The issue with you *may* be the issue of the vodka I mentioned earlier: giving up martinis. "If, for instance, you are in the habit of buying good vodka for your martini . . . make an accounting of your liquor bill and the money you save on it and turn it over to another cause." You would be surprised at the amount you can turn over. Be honest. A cocktail in this city can cost $4.50. Two makes $9.00. Make it a round ten, for the tips. Multiply that by six, and then by the five weeks of Lent, and you have a tidy sum: three hundred dollars. I tell you about it this way because I do it this way. It hurts a lot: the tender part, the pocket. And this can go to the Choir School Soup Kitchen which the choristers help administer when they distribute the food and sandwiches they have made on Saturday mornings.

I tell you this because I have done exactly that again this year. And here it is. Apart from the fact that this hurts, this really will ensure my Lenten observance in this one particular regard, because there *is* no more money readily available for this commodity. I've been and gone and cut off the source. You can do the same thing with money saved from a meal in a restaurant.

Lent is a time for keeping friendships in repair. That may mean the discipline of letter writing or some visits or some regular telephone calls to a lonely person in your life who may or may not welcome the initiative you take. For the love of Christ do something about the neglected soul, or have a shot at reconciliation with somebody with whom you've had a difference or a separation. Try forgiving. That is more costly than six weeks of vodka. Better still, try both. I have somebody in mind whose friendship I need to pay attention to. That's the next job.

What about making your confession? That is as expensive to your pride as the check for vodka is to your pocket. You know how to prepare for a confession? List the seven deadly sins on a piece of paper — preferably a large piece, a legal pad. Under the headings put the circumstance. Don't euphemize. If it's stealing, don't refer to it as borrowing.

It may come as a surprise to you when I ask if you have ever made a retreat. A weekend of silent reflection and worship, of Scripture meditation and of listening for God may be something you had never for a moment contemplated. You might well rethink that. Or ask the clergy for the title of a book to tackle. For those of you who don't have much opportunity or propensity for reading, *that* discipline may be just as costly, and just as bracing. Flexing neglected muscles can be rewarding once you have got over the discomfort. The secret is that you have to keep those muscles toned up. It may open up for you a part of life that can be a real joy in its discovery. Christ's joy can come to a soul when it loses itself in wonder. Reading can assist that. And your own worship can benefit from it.

I want to finish by again saying that observance of Lent involves embracing projects both personal and altruistic; we have biblical warrant for that. It is not so much a time for thinking as for welcoming an opportunity to "grow into the measure of the stature of the fullness of Christ," whose glory is our joy and whose joy is our glory and our great reward.

Everything Must Go

Parables run through the streets of Manhattan like sparks through stubble. I pass shop windows every day on my way to work and pray here that say "Everything Must Go." Everything must go. Apply that to yourself, and you will be well on the way to realizing what the season of Lent is about. Lent is a time of departure, of letting go, of severance, *and of new stock;* it is a time of welcoming new styles, new ways of looking at things, new ways of wearing things, often in a new location.

A word very often aligned with what God is and what he does and how he does things is the term *new.* He claims he makes all things new. That really is the message of Easter, and on Easter Day you will be hearing that in the events in which he has worked mightily with his Son for us and for our salvation. But from creation onward, the testimony of the people who own him and love him as Lord and God in their lives has been that he is associated with newness by creating newness, re-creating in new ways, providing the universe and all humanity on this planet with access to freshness, to "newness of life," as the old Prayer Book calls it. But the newness of God's activity among us isn't cosmetic. It isn't a matter of putting together a cover from bits and pieces or of disguising the brokenness with a shiny coat of enamel: the divine activity isn't to be confused with the

59

antique porcelain restoration business. Everything must go first.

You heard the first Lesson. It is the story of the new covenant. The world had seen the flood, the divine judgment upon the world's apostasy and sin. Everything had to go; and, in fact, everything went in that flood, that deluge, except the people chosen to be the instruments of the new work God had planned for his creation, and with them he instituted that lovely covenant and promises:

> And I will establish my covenant with you; neither shall all flesh be cut off any more by the waters of a flood; neither shall there any more be a flood to destroy the earth. And God said, This is the token of the covenant which I make between me and you . . . for the perpetual generations: I do set my bow in the cloud . . . and I will look upon it, that I may remember.

> Genesis 9:11-16, KJV

Everything had to go. When it went, God created a new arena for his activity, and the sign of it was one of the loveliest phenomena in the created order, about which poets have sung and which painters have portrayed: the rainbow, which is the newest thing to be seen after the darkness of thunder and rain and devastation have departed, the symbol of a new peace, the symbol of fresh hope, fragile indeed, and soon to disappear, only to be seen again in some different place, encompassing all the imaginable colors of light, embracing all the beauty of which humanity can conceive, the eternal newness and freshness of God himself, and in its shape eternally symbolic of him who is without beginning and without end.

St. Paul, who knew this covenant and this story as "a Hebrew born and bred, in . . . attitude to the law, a Pharisee; . . . in legal rectitude, faultless," as he said in his letter to the church at Philippi, knew the truth of this in his own life. Everything had to go. His Pharisaism, his legalism, his chauvinism, his elitism — it all had to go. Listen again to the magnificent words that emphasize this:

> But all such assets I have written off because of Christ. I would say more: I count everything sheer loss, because all is far outweighed by the gain of knowing Christ Jesus my Lord, for whose sake I did in fact lose everything. I count it so much garbage, for the sake of gaining Christ and finding myself incorporate in him, with no righteousness of my own, no legal rectitude, but the righteousness which comes from faith in Christ, given by God in response to faith. All I care for is to know Christ, to experience the power of his resurrection, and to share in his sufferings, in growing conformity with his death, if only I may finally arrive at the resurrection from the dead.
>
> Philippians 3:8-11, NEB

Christ was why everything in Paul's life had to go. The ancient story was being retold in the life of the Pharisee, Saul of Tarsus, who in legal rectitude had considered himself faultless. Then there had come the catastrophe, the cataclysm in his life of self-confident and arrogant persecution of the church. As with sudden thunder and the flood upon the earth, the thunder of God had sounded as he was on his murderous errand to Damascus. Darkness followed with his blindness, and then there came the new covenant. Christ is the rainbow, the light in this covenant, and Saul comes back as Paul. As he later wrote in a letter to the Colossians, he had put on the new man.

That confrontation, that cataclysm, that turning again to God in Christ is known by a term in the Church: penitence, *metanoia*. "Turn back O man, *forswear* thy foolish ways" — the garbage to which Paul relegates them: the habit of thinking I can't possibly be wrong, the habit of thinking myself in legal and moral rectitude faultless, and other foolish patterns of selfishness and self-satisfaction.

Create in me a new heart, O God;
Renew a right spirit within me.

The work of creation and renewal will only begin, can only begin, when I turn my face to the Lord and lay bare the accoutrements which cover the heart. Christ will not perform his surgery upon me if I keep my back to him, my face buried in the mattress of my selfishness and pride. And it is not a general anesthetic that he gives; we have to watch his eyes as his hands work upon us patiently and painfully, for there are wounds made by nails in them. The work when once begun, the divine surgery, will never end — at least, until he is finished, and who are we to assume that he has done with us all that needs to be done? We place ourselves in his hands when we turn to face him, and the great adventure has begun as we watch his eyes.

That confrontation, that eye-watching, is applied by some souls in the practice of *confession,* because frankness and honesty are prime requisites of eye-watching. Without hysteria, without excuses, without circumlocution, the heart that has been turned to Christ will recount its various failures and betrayals. Let us make a systematic approach to penitence.

Get a piece of paper and, if you are realistic, reach for a large sheet. Make seven headings, the seven cardinal sins, or deadly sins: pride, anger, sloth, envy, lust, gluttony, and hatred. Under each heading, note the occasions you failed God. Don't fudge; don't find excuses; don't blame and don't euphemize. If you have stolen, put it under envy. If you have slandered someone's character, put it under hatred. If you have committed adultery, you know where to write that. If you can't categorize it, put it under pride. Pride is the catchall category for all that we can't get right as we strive to "be as gods." Remember that envy isn't merely wanting something very badly that you haven't got: it is resenting somebody else's having it. Make a clean breast of it. Keep the list and sleep on it. Add to it as you turn up memories of past wrongs, persistent wrongs, your familiar sins, what John Donne calls "whispering sins," even what you thought in your pride were your cherished strengths and righteousnesses but which put others in a poorer light. Then do one of two things. Take yourself, take your list, to a priest and in secret recite it, sparing yourself nothing and knowing that another penitent sinner who knows God's forgiveness is listening merely in order to help you clarify a doubt in your mind or gently to help you face a situation you can hardly bear to name, and who at the end of it will pronounce God's forgiveness over you, the channel of the grace and the minister of the sacrament. Or take yourself to some quiet place and kneel and read your list aloud to God, alone and in secret. It is the facing and naming of the things in which you have failed God that brings you to a state where God can make his new covenant with you: his forgiveness, his life henceforth to be lived in you. In that covenant, Christ's life in you is the rainbow, the light, and like Saul you come back a new man, a child of God restored to the image of himself, which has been his plan for you since all eternity, before the worlds began. Paul knew it, and so can you.

> It is not to be thought that I have already achieved . . . perfection, but I press on, hoping to take hold of that for which Christ once took hold of me. My friends, I do not reckon myself to have got hold of it yet. All I can say is this: forgetting what is behind me, and reaching out for that which lies ahead, I press towards the goal to win the prize which is God's call to the life above, in Christ Jesus.

> Philippians 3:12-14, NEB

In that forgetting — *for everything must go,* in the newness of life in Christ — Paul's song echoes a mysterious tune sounded by Isaiah the prophet. Reminding his people of the covenant once made with them that everything must go, Isaiah writes of God as saying:

> Remember ye not the former things, neither consider the things of old. Behold, I will do a new thing.

Isaiah 43:18-19, KJV

Take It All Off!

Have you noticed in the papers the number of photographs illustrating health and sports clubs? On two facing pages in Monday's copy of the *New York Times* there appear two advertisements for the Club La Racquette, and Apple Health and Sports Club, respectively. Healthy bodies without much on. And the two advertisement titles? "Take 50% Off" and "Take It All Off." Take what off? I wasn't quite sure, but I discovered it referred to the membership rates.

I am sure about one thing. Working out is *work*. Working out takes a lot of self-discipline. But people cheerfully undertake the painful and sweaty regimen and rejoice to feel better as a result. Perhaps they hope for the body in the *New York Times* photographs. Perhaps romance will come if they look fitter. Whatever the motive, health clubs flourish and propagate as people not only take off some percentage of the club rates but excess fat here and there.

They also take something on. Muscle. Ash Wednesday is the day of days for signing up not at a health class but at a *wholeness* class. It is a time of training and exercise for the soul. It is sweaty, sustained effort, bent on reducing soul fat and building heart muscle. "Create in me a clean heart, O God; and renew a right spirit within me" (Ps. 51:10, KJV). That is how the psalmist puts it.

You can use the advertisement title for your motto if you like: "Take it all off." The concealed lazinesses we indulge in. The little dishonesties regarding time and money that we practice. The secret treacheries to people we are committed to. The selfish vanities we cherish about ourselves. The high-sounding stinginesses we maintain. The Christian love we withhold, and the resentments we nurture. All this flab around the thighs of our life's progress. Take it all off!

And let Christ do the massaging. Begin with the ashes of repentance. Say you're sorry. It hurts him to manhandle you because there are wounds in his hands. But he will do it for love of you, and as he works on you his eyes will never wander from yours, so there is no hope of evasion or excuse. It will be uncomfortable. But in the end you will be able to say with the psalmist, "Thy hands have made me and fashioned me" (Ps. 119:73, KJV) as you emerge sore and less steady on your self-confident feet, having submitted to his discipline, and grown, by his grace alone, a little, "unto the measure of the stature of the fulness of Christ" (Eph. 4:13, KJV).

Cholesterol of the Soul

Some of us have trouble with our cholesterol level. You are looking at an example. The experts tell us that the low density level is dangerous when it is high and the high density level ought not to be low. Pull one down; push the other up. How? Discipline. You don't eat this, you don't touch that. Gone are the things you like to eat best. Gone, but not forgotten. But the inducement to avoiding the temptation is not to look better but to stay alive and be able to function freely, so you turn away. You say no. You reach for what you know will make you free, and in the future, grateful. Your heart will be sounder for it all, because your blood will be able to get around in arteries that aren't clogged up.

If you think you are free from a cholesterol problem, I have news for you: there is cholesterol of the soul. The arteries of the soul need God's life to flood them, to keep the soul truly alive and functioning vigorously. But the fatty accretions of self, those insidious hidden little selfishnesses and self-indulgences and excuses for your tiny dishonesties and resentments and nurtured grievances, your whispering sins, as John Donne calls them, those sneaky self-justifications for getting away with things less than honorable, the half-truths told, the truths uttered in order to hurt the listener, the tiny jabs of malice, the snobberies and the self-satisfactions we like to be massaged with — what about all those things? They don't just evaporate into nothingness; they gum up the arteries of the soul. Cholesterol of the spirit. They build up unseen and unsuspected, and love, which is the life of God in us, has a hard time getting around. It could cease to flow altogether.

Lent is the time for a check-up. Ash Wednesday is when we come to the Physician of our souls, our Maker and Redeemer, and for every single one of us there is a poor report, *an alarming diagnosis.* We've all got cholesterol of the spirit. In the Old Testament there is a phrase: "hearts as fat as brawn." It means the same thing. Thank God for this annual check-up, Ash Wednesday. We start the diet. Penitence. Saying you're sorry: *ashes.* Acknowledging the presence of cholesterol in our soul's arteries. We consider the diet, purpose to amend our lives, express a determination to turn away from the cream of putting self first, from the red meats of our selfish lusts and illicit passions, from the fats on which our mean sides slide.

But cleaning up our act requires more than cutting things out. We must also avail ourselves of the cleansing power of preparing for the sacraments more carefully and partaking of them more frequently, the astringent treatment of some Bible reading and study to get the brain end of the soul working and exercising, to lubricate the generosities of heart and hand, with an eye to others less fortunate who should be the beneficiaries of our regimen and diet in Lent. Find a project, a single project, to support: the homeless or AIDS victims, some work of mercy.

The secret is allowing God to do his work in us. Let go and let God, as one of my colleagues puts it. Only he can dislodge the cholesterol we build up in our souls with our selfishnesses. The treatment is painful. Make no mistake about it. And never-ending. But your aim, as mine, for our eternal life's sake is to be able to say with St. Paul,

Nevertheless I live: but it is Christ who lives in me!

Galatians 2:20

Forget It?

We have a dismissive phrase in Manhattan and elsewhere: Forget it! It implies that the cause is hopeless or the subject preposterous or the project outrageous. Forget it. Put it right out of your mind. It is a rude suggestion to change the subject or abandon the quest.

But this is the day when we can't say forget it. This is the day when we remember it. *It* is the need to say sorry to God. Sorry for having neglected him, not having taken the trouble and the time to go to worship him or to listen to what we know he is saying through the lives of people who really love him and can't help but bring their goodness and their standards among the muddle and the mess of our own existence. Sorry to God for having flown in the face of what we know he wants from us: truth, generosity, humility, obedience. This is the day when we remember it.

It is the day when we take a look in the mirror. The trouble is that we have skated along the thin edge between truth and half-truth and untruth so adeptly that we can hardly recognize ourselves for what we are anymore. But Ash Wednesday is the day when with lesser or greater accuracy we catch sight of ourselves — and resolve to do something about it. Not in order to make ourselves feel good, but in hopes of having our relationship with God renewed, restored to where we know uncomfortably if uncertainly it should be. And what we can see of ourselves in the mirror isn't reassuring. We are curiously fat from too much self-indulgence, self-will, self-assurance. And our looks have faded — into indifference, into compromise with our lesser selves and lower standards, into settling for second best in the way we deal with ourselves and others. Our faces have fallen into unworthy despair and acquiescence in situations that in our better moments we would never have allowed ourselves to accept, into settling for easy options in order to avoid unpleasantness and difficult situations. We face a sorry image in the mirror.

Facing all this, we don't think of *forgetting it* on Ash Wednesday. We face it. Which is why you are here. You realize that, as the words of Scripture we heard read this morning put it, "*now* is the time." Now is the time for the Holy Spirit to restore us into the image of God. He offers his forgiveness, the gift of himself in Christ's body and blood. He offers to be at our elbow as we make that dangerous turn on the thin ice, skating to truth from between half-truth and untruth. That turn, that dangerous turn on thin ice, is called *metanoia,* repentance, when you turn to the Lord to be saved.

Now, as you sit there, renew your act of repentance. Say you're sorry. Ask for God's help on that turn from untruth to truth; ask for his arm on your elbow. Make the turn. Do it now. Tell him you're sorry. Ask his help. Turn. And *then* you can say forget it. But not before. I'll tell you why. St. Paul says so. After he made the turn, he said,

> Forgetting what is behind me, and reaching out for that which lies ahead, I press towards the goal to win the prize which is God's call to the life above, in Christ Jesus.

> Philippians 3:13-14, NEB

Fears Facing a Christian: Sickness

Some of you will have met a woman in my life with a large smile, a large figure, and a large personality. She served for thirteen years as my housekeeper and cook, Lonnie Belle Gay. She had a friend who also worked on Park Avenue, called Skinny Minnie, with the same vital statistics. Her employer one day asked for the dining room chandelier to be washed. So a pail of soapy water was placed on the dining room table, and Skinny Minnie climbed on. There was a groan and a crash as the table collapsed, and the next thing she saw was the ceiling as she was lying on her back looking up at the chandelier in a pool of soapy water and broken pedestals. She telephoned Lonnie. Lonnie said, "Where are your shoes?" "Here." "Honey, start runnin'."

This story ended happily because the employer returned just as Skinny Minnie fled and chased her down Park Avenue. "Get back. Clean up the mess. We can mend a table. You can't mend a situation by running away from it."

Nor can you. There are no such things as running shoes for evading distress or pain in the Christian faith and life. Things we don't always want to cope with have to be met, whether we have caused them or not. And this Lent we are trying to consider fears that a Christian may have to face and the way we can face these fears, for Christ's own sake.

There are things in the world that we are sure will

never happen to us. While we are young, vigorous, and, to a greater or lesser extent, attractive, we consider ourselves immune to any number of things. Old age and death remain spots on a distant horizon, and so long as we are healthy, how many of us give a thought to sickness — sickness of the sort that can leave its mark upon us, if ever it leaves us at all? You go blithely to your long-neglected doctor. You feel thankfully unfamiliar with the waiting room as you eye the others sitting there. Some look bedraggled, some confident, like you. Some have fear in their eyes; others look as though hope has flown out of the window. You have a routine physical, your blood is taken, and you forget about the whole thing. Then the telephone rings and the doctor's nurse is asking you to come round sooner rather than later: the doctor would like to see you. Gently the news is broken to you. The thing that will never happen to you has happened. Without a twinge of pain, without missing a heartbeat, without a trace of anything you noticed, something has changed from going right to going wrong. There is a sudden hole in your stomach as you fall out of your familiar world into another, a world lower than the one you took for granted: less sunshine, less music, more walls and barriers, and a sort of telling silence in which you can hear your heart beat.

More tests. More waiting. Then the news. What do you say and how do you say it to your lover, the person who shares your life, your partner, the "wife of your bosom," as the Scriptures say? How do you put it so that the other won't fall apart, so that you don't end up having to support your supporter? The mind works in two ways. The crushing news numbs you and sequential thought eludes you; then a kaleidoscope of memories and strategies flashes in front of you as you close the doctor's door behind you. Irrational hope, irrational denial, irrational blame well up in the street you tread like bursting water mains. You had set out without a care. You come back with a vulture perching on your shoulder.

No human is exempt from this possibility. There is in the gospel of Christ no protective door you can close to separate it from you. In fact, it is the other way around.

There are certain givens with which Christians have to work. The first is that sickness is not, nor ever can be, ascribed as divine *punishment* for sin. No person has the right to attribute to God an act that, perforce, falls into the category of *human* vengeance, retaliation, vindictiveness, or caprice. When people do make such ascriptions, they are making God over in their own image, and a shoddy and detestable image it is, a rotten caricature, a defilement of the perfect love that gives life to the world. For "all have sinned and fallen short of the glory of God," and by that spiteful yardstick nobody at all would enjoy good health; we should all be invalids.

The second given is that some forms of sickness *are* your own fault, the inevitable consequence of actions taken heedlessly, accidentally, or deliberately. Sin *can* be an ingredient in the mixture. Sexual promiscuity invites diseases, some of them killers. Taking foolish risks with bad weather, being impatient with traffic, indulging in gluttony, taking unlawful drugs, immoderately consuming alcohol — there is a whole catalogue of avoidable injuries that can be charged to arrogance and self-will. We all know when we have, as we say, "tempted fate," and as Christians we should know it clearly. So no self-pity! There is a pungent verse in the first letter of Peter. "What credit is there in fortitude when you have done wrong and are beaten for it? But when you have behaved well and suffer for it, your fortitude is a fine thing in the sight of God" (1 Pet. 2:20, NEB).

The third given is how Christ deals with the sick: he makes them well. The Gospels tell us that "when the sun was setting, all they that had any sick . . . brought them unto him; and he laid his hands on every one of them, and healed them" (Luke 4:40, KJV).

Yes. We know that verse. But do you realize what is really going on? Matthew records that a paralytic man was brought to him, and "seeing their faith Jesus said to the man, 'Take heart, my son; your sins are forgiven'" (Matt. 9:2, NEB). Aren't you surprised? Wouldn't you have expected Jesus to heal him first and then to absolve him from whatever sin was there? Jesus does not explain. He looks, and he knows what he must do to *save* this paralytic.

Examine Christ's scale of priorities. The first is not necessarily physical wholeness: it is holiness. This is disconcerting, because in our preoccupation with physical health we are inclined to make wholeness preeminent. Christ's mission is salvation, nothing less. That involves the redemption not merely of physical failure and mental malaise but the whole world of creation, physical and spiritual. This cosmic concept is stupendous, and human wholeness is part of it. But only part. Christ's concern here with holiness before wholeness is part of it. But only part. Christ's concern here with holiness before wholeness brings a bewildering realm of priorities to our notice, the divine priorities. He takes a man and exposes him first to divine forgiveness. The depths of that experience, as well we know, cannot be plumbed, for we are dealing with the mystery of the divine holiness and its standards, and all language to describe it limps and staggers. Poetry may go further. Liken it, as the prophet-poet of old did, to a *refiner's fire,* which reduces to dust and dross all human pretense, all human pride, all human failure, leaving the object purified as well as reduced.

He absolves the paralytic. An ancient saint, Theophilus Bishop of Antioch, declared,

> Hear further, O man, *the work of the resurrection going on in yourself;* even though you are unaware of it. For perhaps

you have sometimes fallen sick, and lost flesh, and strength, and beauty, but *when you received again from God mercy and healing* — mercy and healing — you picked up again in flesh and appearance and recovered your strength.

Holiness before wholeness. In the way Christ deals with the sick, he opens a window into the mystery of cosmic salvation. Put it another way. What you see is what you can see of an iceberg: there is a hidden mountain of God's life and purpose under the surface. We are permitted through his act of healing a glimpse at something of the awesomely vast divine activity, of which healing is a part.

So then, for a Christian there is a series of perspectives in which sickness plays a part: divine perspectives. When you are sick and the priest comes to you to give you your communion, he is conveying Christ's healing in Christ's own terms, and thereby reinforcing the divine priorities: the divine life in the blessed sacrament forgives as it feeds as it supports the divine skills of the doctors and surgeons who are working on you. Remember that the doctors' skills are part of that vast mysterious machinery of the redemptive process, and be thankful for them and for the people called to use them.

Then there is a fourth given. It is difficult and complex — difficult for me to talk about, standing in front of you and, thanks to the skills of my doctor, enjoying good health. I don't want to be that horrible cleric who preaches glib sermons. The fourth given has to do with how we cope with the suffering that sickness can bring. The testimony of those holy people who have suffered is that God is somehow with them in the suffering. You may remember the Old Testament story of the pagan King Nebuchadnezzar, who threw three of God's brave servants, Shadrach, Meshach, and Abednego, into the fiery furnace and, when he looked in to see, discovered "*four* men loose, walking in the midst of the fire, and they have no hurt; and the form of the fourth is like the Son of God" (Dan. 3:25, KJV). This discovery has been the possession of people for whom God is very much a reality in their lives — that God is somehow with them even in the isolation of their pain. It makes for a curious and very brave form of acceptance that carries them in a mysterious peace. Someone we are acquainted with knew this peace. St. Paul was an invalid. He had a chronic complaint which he called the thorn in his side. What it was we do not know. It might have been psychological. My guess is that with his dyspeptic personality it might have been a duodenal ulcer the size of a tennis ball. He says quite frankly that he prayed to be healed three times and was told, "My Grace is sufficient for Thee." Holiness before wholeness. He it was who wrote, "Suffering begets endurance. Endurance begets character. Character begets hope, hope which will never be disappointed" (Rom. 5:3). He achieved peace with this acceptance. He could say, "If I glory I must needs glory in my infirmities" (2 Cor. 12:5). Acceptance. Listen now to this, by Amy Carmichael:

> He said, "I will forget the dying faces
> The empty places —
> They shall be filled again;
> O voices mourning deep within me cease."
> Vain, vain the word: vain, vain;
> Not in forgetting lieth peace.
>
> He said, "I will withdraw me and be quiet,
> Why meddle in earth's riot?
> Shut be my door to pain.
> Desire thou dost befool me; thou shalt cease."
> Vain, vain the word: vain, vain;
> Not in aloofness lieth peace.
>
> He said, "I will submit; I am defeated;
> God hath depleted

My rich life its gain.
O futile murmurings; why will ye not cease?"
Vain, vain the word: vain, vain;
Not in submission lieth peace.

He said, "I will accept the breaking sorrow
Which God tomorrow
Will to His son explain."
Then did the turmoil deep within him cease.
Not vain the word, not vain:
For in acceptance lieth peace.

Fears Facing a Christian: Helplessness

Some weeks ago when I was getting ready to board a plane I spotted a modern-day Mark Twain: grey hat, cream silk suit, looking as though he had stepped off *Showboat*. This man eased himself into the seat in front of me, and I realized I was sitting behind Tom Wolfe, the author of the explosive best-seller *Bonfire of the Vanities*. If you have a strong stomach for a tale with precious little redemption in it, read it. Hilarious as it is, it is merciless, remorseless, and in parts revolting as well as fascinating in its account of this city of Manhattan where everybody is unkind and nobody emerges as a figure whom the author can admire. But what comes through, loud and clear, is the helplessness engulfing an observer of a city teeming with *piranhas*, those small fish with murderous teeth. Come what may, there are few survivors. We are eaten alive, financially, judicially, educationally, politically, because we cannot swim fast enough to evade them.

Helplessness is the fear that daunts some Christians, a dread of not being able to do much to prevent damage, to influence the situations that engulf both us and those we love, situations in which, as my colleague Fr. Robert Stafford says, we are confronted by powerlessness and life's unmanageability. I know we give him a hard time for mentioning this in most of his sermons, but it *is* an issue of great seriousness and the cause of much anxiety and grief to people around us, and perhaps to us as well. They have fears for the future, and their helplessness wells up at what the world seems to be turning into and becoming capable of.

I was recently talking to a young man going through what many a young man experiences: premarriage nerves. He spoke of his reluctance to bring children into a world so uncertain in its future and seemingly so doomed. He felt helpless to shape their environment in any meaningful way, to battle the very evident forces of deterioration. That healthy and resourceful man's name is Legion. There are many of his generation who are appalled at their powerlessness to affect their future. Pessimism is rife because of things like the AIDS epidemic, which threatens to claim millions during the nineties, and the still powerful nuclear threat, which leaves all of us helpless and fearful. How can we not be dispirited by the way world powers play power games, delaying the release of the truth about situations or withholding it altogether?

And as the ache of helplessness increases, our Christian faith is no anodyne, no anesthetic. Just the opposite. The faith we profess heightens rather than dulls our sensitivity to pain and anguish. It helps us see the world more clearly, and when we do, its pains wound us more piercingly. As St. Paul notes in a discussion of the body of Christ in his first letter to the Corinthians, "all its organs . . . feel the same concern for one another. If one organ suffers, they all suffer together" (1 Cor. 12:25-26, NEB).

Consider the helplessness that many Christians experience in confronting a changing church. In their view, the church is leaving her old established landmarks and pressing on into territories not merely uncharted but unimaginable, her liturgies altered, her language scrutinized for sexist content, her hymnals revised, her moralities restated, her marriage laws relaxed, the election of her bishops transformed into political dog-and-pony shows, populism rampant, as reflected in the mediocre standards of her worship, declining congregations, and hordes of unemployed clergy. For some it seems a nightmare becoming reality as the prospect of women bishops emerges for the first time in the history of the Christian church. There is a possibility of a break-up of the Anglican communion, some churches feeling that they may no longer continue in communion with a branch of their church that deals tradition so devastating a blow. And the people experiencing what to them is a nightmare feel absolutely helpless; they have no resources with which to combat this assault upon the structure of their loyalties. It is as though the church were proceeding on automatic pilot, as though the course, having been determined by a hasty democratic vote, is now being pursued with no one at the controls.

This helplessness leads to anger, anger which is difficult to target. It's no good deploring the state of the clergy; I know that they are a disappointing lot, but we have only the laity to choose from. And finding fault with the bishops who have been chosen from the poor-quality clergy has been a favored sport of the church since the fifth century, when someone complained that whereas in former times the bishops were made of gold and the chalices of wood, now there are gold chalices and wooden bishops.

There is much evidence of anger at the church on the part of the people of God partly because they see it languishing in cultural captivity, caving in to clamant secular standards, measuring itself by the world's yardstick, and they simply will not capitulate to such capitulation.

Along with the helplessness you can experience at things happening around you over which you have no control, there are times when you can experience helplessness at things happening *inside* you over which you seem at first to have little or no control. You heard the collect: "Almighty

God who seest that we have no power of ourselves to help ourselves." I'm talking about the inner struggles you face between your better and your worse self. St. Paul was no stranger to this inner struggle, which could leave him paralyzed with helplessness. You heard him say in the portion of his letter to the Romans read as today's epistle,

> For I know that nothing good lodges in me — in my unspiritual nature, I mean — for though the will to do good is there, the deed is not. The good which I want to do, I fail to do. . . . I discover this principle, then: that when I want to do the right, only the wrong is within my reach. In my inmost self I delight in the law of God, but I perceive that there is in my bodily members a different law, fighting against the law that my reason approves and making me a prisoner under the law that is in my members, the law of sin. Miserable creature that I am, who is there to rescue me out of this body doomed to death?

> Romans 7:18-24, NEB

He is trapped, helpless, between what he knows he should do and what he finds he ends up doing, which is nowhere near the standards of his conscience and its expectations. And he writes as though he were constantly disappointed at himself. He describes a condition we all know about. Who of us has not experienced the inner paralysis of motive, wondering whether we do what we do because it's right or because it somehow helps our self-image? Who of us has not fallen into inertia when we know ourselves to be guilty and are torn between the temptation to try to deflect some of the blame and the knowledge that as Christians we must accept responsibility and its attendant humiliation? We know that as "ministers of reconciliation" we should make a heartfelt attempt to reach amity and understanding with people who work with us, and yet it seems so much easier to settle for the status quo of distaste, distance, and dis-

81

respect, even if that means that the reconciliation is never properly won, for God. Who of us has not known writer's block when it comes time to pen a letter to put a situation right, make a person happier, bring hope back, allay anxieties, and convey forgiveness? There are a thousand ways in which we know what to do and find ourselves because of our own selfishness and self-interest deprived of the will to accomplish it. Lent is the time of times to go at these paralyses, because we know where the answer to our problem lies. Paul tells us: "God alone, through Jesus Christ our Lord."

We may stand helpless before the machinations of Manhattan in Tom Wolfe's *Bonfire of the Vanities*. We may be stunned into immobility by what the superpowers threaten to do to each other. We may feel like pawns on a nuclear chessboard. We may be inclined to respond to what the Church seems bent on doing by venting our anger and disgust through withholding our money, withdrawing our support, ceasing to want to learn new ways (and conceivably better ways) of worshiping together, refusing to listen to the challenge of new insights, preferring the old, the familiar, the comfortable, and the undemanding, living in the past and refusing to come out of it. We may feel powerless at things within us that strive to pull the best in us down to mediocrity or even worse. We may feel like giving in to despair and self-pity, forgetting that Christ requires us to love ourselves as well as those around us. All these things can sink our feet into the "mire and clay," as the psalmist says, of forgetting that God is not asleep or away from us, that he has the whole world in his hands, that he is the Lord of the church and he will have his way with it, tinker with it as busy churchmen might, that Christ has promised to be with us to the end of time, his Spirit guiding us, that he lives in us and is working in us to resolve the paralysis with which our temptations assail us. He can do this because of his own obedience to the Father's will, his willingness to offer himself up to death upon the cross, and his power to rise again for us, to claim the sovereignty that is his due.

Paul, as he always can, puts the whole thing in two nutshells: "God was in Christ reconciling the world to himself" (2 Cor. 5:19, NEB). "He is the head, and on him the whole body depends" (Eph. 4:15-16, NEB). He is for us eternally the one of whom the hymn sings: "Help of the helpless, O abide with me!"

Fears Facing a Christian: Old Age

You might well say that antiques are an *acquired taste.* Most people tend to equate the interesting with the new and the novel. A new play, a new face in town, a new dish to eat, a new cocktail to taste, a new book, a new restaurant, a new style — mention one, and people will prick up their ears. Mention Christie's antique porcelain sale next week and people will relegate you to an age beyond theirs: the oldies, to that age when you have lost interest in what's hot in New York. Whereas they have not. They're alive. They're in touch.

It has ever been thus. It was said of the Athenians of old — you can find it in the Acts of the Apostles — that they "and the foreigners who lived there spent their time in nothing except telling or hearing something new" (Acts 17:21, RSV).

There is such a thing as impatience with the old. I happen to have an ancient rug in the rectory dining room, threadbare, patched, and raggedy at the edges. It is, or was, a fine example of its oriental sort, with jewel colors. The fact that it is shabby, patched with obvious patches, doesn't much matter to me, but I had to defend it with my life when the firm who helps with our furniture here gave me a lecture on the benefits of acquiring a bright new specimen. I fear I was relegated to the obsolescents, along with the carpet.

As with things, so with people. There is in this world an impatience with the old, and it begins very young. Do

you want to read a cautionary tale? Open your Bibles to the
second book of the Kings, chapter two, verse 23:

> [Elisha] . . . went up from there to Bethel; and while he was
> going up on the way, some small boys came out of the city
> and jeered at him, saying, 'Go up, you baldhead! Go up, you
> baldhead.' And he turned around, and when he saw them, he
> cursed them in the name of the LORD. And two she-bears came
> out of the woods and tore forty-two of the boys.

2 Kings 2:23-24, RSV

There. That's what can happen when you cheek your elders.

The point here is that there was no respect for age.
Now, old people are aware of this possibility and sensitive
to it. Christian people can fear old age because they know
they can fall prey to to the fleet of foot, be taken advantage
of by the strength of a young will and the swiftness of a
young tongue. The onset of age can be the beginning of a
reproach to them, and sometimes they will take desperate
measures to keep age at bay. I know of one partner in a
relationship who has concealed ten years of his age from his
beloved; he fears he will be loved less, sought after less, lose
the attraction he knows he has. He punishes himself in order
to appear younger than he is. At present he's successful. But
wait. People who embark upon this course find that more
measures will be needed before long. Drastic measures for
some women who resent the aging process: plastic surgery;
unwise measures, such as too much makeup or unsuitable
clothes. Is there anything in the world more disconcerting
than having to greet mutton dressed up as lamb?

This defiance born of vanity is a losing battle, and I
suppose that with all the compassion we can muster for those
defiant souls who fear they have more to lose than is perhaps
the case, we must hope that they might learn to give in
gracefully. Easier said than done, I suppose. But there are
deeper areas of genuine concern and fear for Christians as the

mantle of old age is placed on their shoulders. There is a sense of abandonment often, of being left out on a limb. Take a look at the seventy-first Psalm, *"in Te, Domine, speravi:* in Thee, O Lord, have I put my trust," with its poignant — I almost said *pathetic* — cry of an old psalmist: "I am become as it were a monster unto many. . . . Cast me not away in the time of old age; forsake me not when my strength faileth me. . . . Forsake me not, O God, in mine old age, when I am gray-headed" (Ps. 71:6, 8, 17, BCP). This could well be the senior citizens' psalm. It is not the psalm of the young, with all the world ahead to charm, seduce, and conquer.

Face it. The landscape looks bleak when you become old. Familiar faces, beloved voices, sustaining presences are removed from the horizon. It becomes emptier, with snow obliterating footpaths you were accustomed to follow without thinking. People become less sure of the paths they once took. Gone are the glad certainties of youth in choices, in decisions, in the onrush of love. You don't fall into and out of love so fast and so recklessly; you become harder to persuade, your gambling instincts no longer erupting. No longer do you feel inclined to pursue something "just for the hell of it." More cautious, more tentative, more fearful of falling, in every sense of that term, more anxious to see and perceive so that you don't make a wrong step, more indecisive, more reluctant to trust the advice of the present and more inclined to rely on remembered and well-tried criteria from the past, more suspicious of the motives of others, and sometimes less forgiving — all these are part of the process of becoming old.

If these are the daily signs of living differently, signs we notice in people getting old, there are also hidden changes. *Faith often erodes.* Ardor fades. People can lose great chunks of faith like stone walls crumbling. Often the first thing to go is the belief in life after death. I have noticed this, and it has distressed me that people I have known and loved somehow let this buttressing faith fall into irrelevance. Whether there is an unseen resentment at the failure of the sap of hope to rise within one's self as formerly it did, whether there is a private anger at being separated by death from a beloved partner, whether the emptying of the land-scape of sustaining and comforting lives reduces the soul to helplessness and feeble defiance — whatever it is, people sometimes find that they end up no longer believing what they have always believed about Christ's promises to be with them always, through the ages, and that in his Father's house are many mansions; if it were not so, would he have told us that he goes to prepare a place for us? Think for a moment of the old people you have been close to, and ask yourself if their firm grasp of faith is not loosening and failing pre-cisely in the area where they had tenaciously and sometimes vociferously proclaimed it: life after death. And yet I can also tell you of the woman with whom I sat in hospital, holding her hand as she went through the death agony with cancer in her spine — her long life had seen much tragedy — who suddenly opened her eyes and smiled and said to me, "Is it all going to be as lovely as this?" and then died immediately. Her passage through the valley with its doubts suddenly ended in a sunshine *which I saw* her experience.

Along with all the things that age lets go — mobility perhaps, hearing perhaps, vision perhaps, the ability to sing — along with all these things there can come a clarity of perspective and control of priorities that can be astringently good for the likes of us. In our moralistic way of establishing priorities, it comes as a bit of a shock to hear a saintly woman who loved God and wrote about him very tellingly, Dorothy Sayers, whose own moral life was one of integrity and rectitude — to hear her say at the end of her life:

> The older I get and nearer the tomb
> The less do I question who's sleeping with whom.

Banished is the urge to acquire *things*. In fact, they want to divest themselves of things, to be free of things, often things they have cherished throughout their lives. They prefer warmth to glamour, a cup of tea to a diamond choker, sitting in the springtime sun to attending a prestigious dinner party, and almost anything in the world to a cocktail party with socially prominent and ambitious people.

The old laugh at the antics of yuppiedom, and their laughter is a healthy corrective for us. They smile pityingly at pretension of any sort, because they can spot it and see through it faster than we think. They no longer have time for it, because they are aware that time is on nobody's side, least of all their own. Moreover, they do us a service with their frankness, for they have seen it all and been through it all.

Years ago I told you I should preach on the benefit of having a grandmother or grandfather. The young have access to a unique relationship there. Grandparents are an essential corrective to perspective. There's an axiom for you, coined by your rector at six this morning as he was rewriting this sermon. . . . They can give us insights about God and us. Only an old soul, that same psalmist I quoted, could say, "O what great troubles and adversities hast thou showed me! and yet didst thou turn and refresh me; yea, and broughtest me from the deep of the earth again" (Ps. 71:19, BCP). Here's wisdom from someone who has been through it, who realizes God's unchanging love, unsleeping care:

> For thou, O Lord God, art the thing that I long for: thou art my hope, even from my youth.
> Through thee have I been holden up ever since I was born: thou art he that took me out of my mother's womb: my praise shall be alway of thee.

Psalm 71:4-5, BCP

There is a perspective on suffering, disappointment, and loss which seemed at the time to be the end of the world. It isn't. There is more to experience, more to do, more to suffer, and more to give thanks for. It is the old who can understand deeply and say with the psalmist, "My time is in thy hand."

And never forget that it is John's Gospel, the last of the four, written by an old, old man, that has a sophisticated wisdom, a graceful balance, and superb insights that set it apart as a theological masterpiece of timeless value. All the precision of language lived with over a lifetime, the superb arrangement and order of a mature contemplation through decades of rich memory, all the love distilled from the days of his youth's journey with Jesus and those three unforgettable years in Galilee are poured from his crucible into a work of theological history quite unlike any other account of Christ's life.

An old priest who was Archbishop Michael Ramsey's schoolmaster and later became Dean of the Minster in York enriched many lives — mine included — with the prayers he wrote. Some I say in front of you, and some silently. In his old age he wrote a prayer for old people. Again, a distillation of a life "hid with Christ in God." It is remarkable. Listen.

> O LORD GOD, who leavest us not
>   nor forsakest in the time of age;
> Shew me, as my strength faileth,
>   an even fuller lovelier light of thy glory
>   shining over and about me.
>   *O my soul, give thanks!*
>
> There in that glory, let me find mine,
> Grant me new store of gentleness, gratitude, patience;
>   new learning of the Passion of my Lord;
>   new dignity of Grace.
> Make my life wholly his life: his heart, my heart;
>   his breath, my breath, breathing love
>   to the very end.
>   *O my soul, give thanks!*

My time is in thy hand.
    Be thou my support in weakness,
    my courage in the dark and in pain,
    mine aid, day and night,
    my company in loneliness,
    my rest.
    O my soul, give thanks!

For all that thou takest from me,
    thou givest what is better,
    and guidest to the best.
    O my soul, give thanks!

Be thy love my bed and covering,
    be thy Christ my living Bread;
    thy Spirit, my strength to the end.
Bring me forth, forgiven, loved, and loving,
    son and servant for ever,
    into thy joy.
    O my soul, give thanks!

The Very Rev. Eric Milner-White,
"My God my Glory"

Fears Facing a Christian: Death

What we have been trying to do this Lent is to bring into focus certain areas in which people who are trying to live out their Christian faith experience fears: loneliness, helplessness, sickness, old age. These fears are genuine, pressing, and daunting no less for Christians. How Christ can help us face them is something we have been looking at. Something we know for sure is that Christ never helps us *not* to face them. The faith of a Christian isn't a sort of celestial anesthetic that takes the sting and pain and possibly the humiliation out of an experience that all humanity at one time or another has to submit to. And perhaps it is right on the most ironic Sunday of the Christian year, when we reenact the welcome given by the people of Jerusalem to Christ on the first Palm Sunday, when we carry palms and sing hosannas, that we should dwell for a time on what was occupying the thoughts of our Savior as he was carried on a donkey through the city gates: the inevitability of his approaching death. Nothing better to introduce this whole consideration have I found than the letter written by a tiny child to God which in three sentences holds all the apprehension and all the fascination combined that we evince as Christian human beings when the possibility confronts us. A little boy called Mike writes this:

Dear God:
What is it like when you die?
Nobody will tell me. I just want to know. I don't want to
do it.

> Your friend,
> Mike

There is all the dread that upon growing up we camouflage
as best we can, and as I said last week, we include the aging
process in that, sometimes by plastic surgery as it takes its
toll upon our looks, and sometimes with pitiful subterfuge
at the very end, at the hands of compliant undertakers. The
experience of death is something the world is afraid to touch
but is obsessed with, repelled and fascinated by at one and
the same time. Look how it features in films and stories. It
colors our speech. Look how it shows itself in our Christian
history in Europe and England with the urge in the four-
teenth and fifteenth centuries to build chantries — chapels
where masses for the soul's rest could repeatedly be offered.
Look at medieval tombs — double deck tombs: the notable
in all his finery lying in state, and underneath on the lower
deck, his skeleton. It shows a lopsided Christian view of the
death experience with this obsession, when what Christ has
to say about it all went forgotten. All people wanted was
to know; they didn't want to do it. It was used as a weapon,
to extract obedience, compliance, and it was financially very
profitable to the church in those days.

They are gone. But the basic fear remains. It lurks at the
back of every Christian head. The fear of being forgotten by
God, uncared for by God. The fear that God's control ends at
death's gate. The fear that for all the brave words, there is
extinction. The fear the psalmist had in his breast when he
could ask, and expect the answer, no:

> Dost thou show wonders among the dead,
>   in the land where all things are forgotten?

Shall thy loving-kindness be shown in the dark?
And thy faithfulness in destruction?

Psalm 88:10-11

Remember as we hear this that Jesus knows that psalm, too; knows it, has recited it since boyhood — and himself knows the answer to the question it raises. That answer is different from everything the world could ever have suspected or calculated. That answer is different from what the world of little Mike today, or from what his sophisticated elders want to hear. Christ is about his Father's business. He knows what that business was, and he has spent his life in the pursuit of it from his childhood on, increasing in wisdom as in stature. And now is the day when his business is recognized and welcomed in the city of God, and it involved his looking death right in its dark face, as he prepares to experience the irony of that welcome.

Death's approach begins in fact the night before, with the poignant symbolic gesture that Mary the sister of Martha makes at the supper in Christ's honor at Bethany, as she anoints the feet of Jesus with what John describes as "very costly perfume" whose fragrance filled the house. When the very man who is soon to betray him and give him up to the forces of darkness and death explodes in fury at the waste, Jesus says, "Leave her alone. . . . Let her keep it till the day when she prepares for my burial" (John 12:7, NEB).

Sitting there, listening to him, is Lazarus, whom Jesus had raised from the dead, and his fame has spread because of what Christ had done, so much so that they "came not only to see Jesus but also Lazarus whom he had raised from the dead" (John 12:9, NEB). Can you imagine what is going through Lazarus's mind? Here the irony begins, for Lazarus is to see what happens the following morning, the first Palm Sunday morning, when "the great body of pilgrims who had come to the festival, hearing that Jesus was on the way to

Jerusalem, took palm branches and went out to meet him, shouting, 'Hosanna! Blessings on him who comes in the name of the Lord!'" (John 12:12-13, NEB), he is to see his bringer-back-to-life on his way to death, facing it, having talked about it the night before, facing it in the midst of the crowd that had heard what Jesus had done to *him:* "The people who were present when he called Lazarus out of the tomb and raised him from the dead told what they had seen and heard. That is why the crowd went to meet him" (John 12:17-18, NEB). And Jesus knows it, knows it with everything else in the minds of those who surround him and shout their proclamations of welcome, and those who feared him because of it.

If the imagination stumbles at what must be going through the mind of Lazarus, we have a clue which St. John gives us about what is going through Christ's: "My soul is in turmoil, and what am I to say? Father, save me from this hour. No it was for this that I came to this hour. Father, glorify thy name" (John 12:27, NEB). Beneath the serenity evident in the face of Christ as he accepts the welcome and the proclamation of his kingship, there is an acceptance of another kind: acceptance of human apprehension as the dark clouds gathered round him, the loneliness which the approach of death brings with it to the solitary soul, for dying is not a group activity, and nobody can shoulder the burden for you — its quiet inevitability, its certainty, its deliberate speed, and its effectiveness. Its effectiveness. He goes on to emphasize its effectiveness: "A grain of wheat remains a solitary grain unless it falls into the ground and dies; but if it dies, it bears a rich harvest" (John 12:24, NEB).

For him then, there is no other way. He has to give himself to it; there can be no avoiding it. "Father, save me from this hour? No. It was for this that I came to this hour." "This" is the final seal he must append to the document of obedience to the Father's will. The writing is in his own blood. But it is the last kiss of trust, for his is the rich harvest to be reaped, and he knows it, and he can say, "Father, glorify thy name."

And he goes on to say something else, about you and me. For true life in him, there has to be true death: the solitary grain of wheat has to fall into the ground and die; it has to experience that solitary experience so as to be solitary no more. There has to be the last surrender. There has to be a falling. We must allow ourselves to be dropped from the hand of a faithful and loving Creator into the good earth of his caring, knowing that all things are in his hands, grain and resting place alike. When we allow it, he can act mightily. For herein lies his promise, that remarkable promise Christ makes precisely at this point: "Where I am, my servant will be." Companionship, Christ's companionship, is promised to the true disciple, for "if anyone serves me, he must follow me" (John 12:26, NEB). There is no other way. There is no shortcut. We look at him, where he is, for he has "gone before," tasted that experience, drunk that chalice of suffering to its dregs, and glorified God's name by his trust, by the obedience he showed in asking his Father to take his Spirit into his hands. And we must follow him in that trust. For he bids us follow him to death — *through* death, to the experience of resurrection life, the life that is "more abundant" which he promises. If you believe that Christ is your Savior and Redeemer, you have to believe this. Redemption in plain language means many things including effecting security, and in the simplest language can mean "making better." The death experience is part of the bettering process.

This lies at the back of the thinking of a woman who has devoted her life to death, to the approach of it and the experience of it and the pain of it and the loneliness of it, in a thousand thousand souls whom she and her companions have sought out and rescued and loved into the next world.

The death of the starving and the poor is a daily reality to this woman, for it is her daily work and her life's task — Mother Teresa of Calcutta. She it is who can say,

> Death is *going home,* yet people are afraid of what will come so they do not want to die. If we do, there is no mystery, we will not be afraid. . . . Death is nothing but a continuation of life, the completion of life. The surrendering of the human body. But the heart and soul live for ever. They do not die. . . . If it were properly explained that death is nothing but going home to God, then there would be no fear.

For Christ has made it better. At the risk of embarrassing my sister Anne, who is having to listen to this while worshiping with us this morning, I want to quote an answer she gave off the top of her head to my father, who was to die a few hours later of cancer in 1971 when he asked her a final question, a question it may occur to you to have thought of asking: "How shall I know when I'm dead?"

"Why, darling, it's when you know and feel you're *completely better.*"

Christ's Encounter with Martha and Mary

Martha and Mary: they have been the comic revue sketch in the drama of the Gospels for centuries. What Mutt and Jeff are for us, what Tom the cat and Jerry the mouse are in the movie cartoons, what Laurel and Hardy were for our parents and grandparents in the late twenties and early thirties, Martha and Mary are for the church. They provide in the gospel what the French term an *entremets* between serious dishes at a grand dinner: a light relief for the palate. Just so in the Gospel of St. Luke: between the glorious parable of the Good Samaritan, with its deathless cogency, and the eternally significant teaching of the Lord's Prayer, known to every Christian who has lived, we find Martha and Mary, and Christ trapped between them — each as strong-minded as the other, each her own woman, each choosing to look at the same thing from the opposite way, each insisting on the correctness of her point of view.

Christ himself was not unaware of the situation, you may be sure, and of the amusing side of it: the doer and the listener, the practical one and the passive one. We must hear the story again for the nuances in the telling of it.

> While they were on their way Jesus came to a village where a woman named Martha made him welcome in her home. She had a sister, Mary, who seated herself at the Lord's feet and stayed there listening to his words. Now Martha was dis-

tracted by her many tasks, so she came to him and said, 'Lord, do you not care that my sister has left me to get on with the work by myself? Tell her to come and lend a hand.' But the Lord answered, 'Martha, Martha, you are fretting and fussing about so many things; but one thing is necessary. The part that Mary has chosen is best; and it shall not be taken away from her.'

Luke 10:38-42, NEB

In the first place, Martha "made him welcome in *her* home": she is the proprietor, and as such she exercises proprietorial rights. She owns the place. At least she acts as though she owns the place. She welcomes visitors. She introduces her family to the visitors. She introduces Mary. Mary is content to be introduced. But Jesus is no stranger. He has known them both some time. He is a beloved friend, a valued and adored person in their lives. He has been with them through thick and thin. Their brother Lazarus had been sick unto death. He had died. Jesus had been told and made his way to see them. Martha had gone to meet him on the way. She had told Mary to stay home and mind the house. Christ had sent for Mary after Martha had told him that her brother would not have died if Jesus had been there. Mary had obeyed his summons. St. John tells us that she had left the house quickly to join him. This beloved man had called their brother out of his grave. He had brought Lazarus back from the dead. The two sisters owed him that.

And now he comes to see them. Martha is ready for him, with a meal that requires the attention you give when an important guest is coming. Everything has to be right. The plates warmed, the meat done to a turn. The wine ready. The places set. This takes time. I know: I do it a lot. I like doing it. I imagine you do, too. Getting ready for a dinner can be a chore if the person who comes is uninteresting or a bore. But when a friend comes!

Jesus comes into a home he is familiar with, to friends he loves and understands. He knows Martha's executive manner; he was exposed to it during the business with Lazarus. He greets her quiet sister, the thoughtful one who possibly prays more and says less. Together they sit and talk while Martha attends to the details. This is the way she wants it. She likes to get things done. Executives do.

But Mary the listener has Christ's attention. He does what a rabbi does: he teaches. And Mary, we are told, sits at his feet, taking it all in. She is a disciple. She wants to learn. It could be that Jesus, immersed in conversation and teaching, fails to throw complimentary remarks over his shoulder through the door into the kitchen about the appetizing smells coming from the oven. Martha chafes at the lack of attention to what she is doing, to the hard work she is putting in; she resents the absorption of the teacher and disciple.

And so she breaks into the conversation. The Scripture says that *she stands over them*. Imagine it. Hot and hair untidy, arms akimbo, she chides Christ: "Lord, *don't you care* that my sister left me alone to do the serving?" "Don't you care?" That is an unfair accusation, ignited by a spark of self-pity. It's the dart we hurl at God when things go wrong for us and we feel sorry for ourselves. We have done this to God and to each other from time immemorial. You hear it in the Psalms: "Wherefore art thou absent from us so long?" "Up, Lord! Why sleepest thou?" "Don't you care?" But listen again: "Don't you care that my sister has left me alone to do the serving?" Martha's complaint has two jabs in it: "Don't *you* care?" — she assumes he doesn't — "that my sister has left me alone to do the serving" — a jab at Mary. Envy.

Envy is when you may be content not to have or be something, but you can't help resenting somebody else having or being it. Martha wants to do the work, prides herself in doing it, rather than sitting around listening to a friend talk. But she becomes angry when her sister who is not encouraged to work enjoys sitting and talking instead.

This is the hidden bit in this story: Martha's envy. It reduces Martha. And it points out the residual temptations awaiting all activists: envy and self-pity. When the church becomes obsessed with its activism, its need to be up and doing, when its perspectives begin to blur the truth that there is such a thing as the dimension of the eternal that has to be remembered in its calculations — when the church forgets as often it does that it is God's church, not the church of 1990s' Manhattan, not the church of the diocese of New York, not the church of the General Convention, not the church of the black caucus or the church of any pressure group or political lobby, then you may be sure that in the flurry of the activity, in the heat and steam of contemporary and clamant issues, exhaustion will overtake it, and it will begin to fall into envy and self-pity and recriminations. You can see it writ large in the church's recent history. You can see it writ small in individual Christian lives, in individual priests and laypeople who have forgotten the dimension of the eternal in the clamor of contemporary involvement with issues and have emerged burned out, exhausted, resentful, and angry at others for failing to care as they care.

Christ is on to Martha's problem and predicament instantly. He warns his good friend and exhausted host: "Martha, Martha!" He reminds her who she is. He does for her what a very good old friend of mine did to me when I lost my temper with him in a restaurant: he told me I was not being at my best. That pulled me around. He was reminding me who I am. "You are fretting and fussing about so many things; but one thing is necessary." One thing. What do you think that one thing might be?

The very thing I have been trying to tell you: Martha forgot the dimension that Mary was aware of. Mary sat and listened. Christ was not talking about the weather or the odds in some upcoming athletic event or even scandals among the Sanhedrin, the church's parliament of the day. He was talking about the reality of God making itself felt in the world of men and women like you and me. He was taking Mary into his confidence about his work, his destiny, his place in the divine Father's plan, the love they shared, and Jesus' duty to say what his Father in heaven wished said to the world. Martha forgot that the part which Mary had chosen was best, and Jesus said so. Martha had not only forgotten, but, like all exhausted activists, she *resented* that side, the quiet, passive side that recognizes the necessity of listening, the necessity of contemplation and quiet in dealing with the things of the hidden God.

Some people and scholars commenting on this passage of Scripture have interpreted Christ's answer as a rebuke to Martha. I would suggest that it was not so much a rebuke as a *reminder*. He recalled her to her destiny.

As he recalls us to ours. There is a part which is best in our commitment to him, a part that will not be taken away from us, a part that is ours eternally. It is within the sanctuary of the soul: to maintain a listening ear as we do the work God gives us to do, to be on the *qui vive*, alert and alive to the divine hints and nudges as we immerse ourselves, sometimes with self-importance and sometimes with self-will, in our determination to serve God. Remember the words of the Psalmist: "Lo, I come to do *thy will*, O LORD; I am content to do it; yea *thy law is within my heart*."

And beloved old Archbishop Michael Ramsey would want me to end with a favorite phrase of his taken from St. Augustine: "A Christian has two eyes; one on the things of earth and one on the things of heaven; and both open, and alert."

The Man from Down Under

Actions, we are told, speak louder than words. Tonight you can see how true that is. From the darkness a light appears. It grows in strength as fire is passed from flame to flame until in the end the place is full of light, and the Easter light surrounds us.

Ask yourself where that light comes from. Not from a shooting star, dipping from the heavens. Not from the wand of some mighty magician, waved benignly from above. *It comes from the earth itself,* the darkness of a place within the earth, the tomb. It comes from down under.

People have always been suspicious of the dark earth, have feared it, have avoided it unless the situation was desperate, and then they burrow into it only for temporary escape and climb out again as soon as possible. They associate it with burial, and they fear above all else being buried alive in it. It signifies the silence and stillness and cold of death.

That light, carried high in the darkness in this great church, is the light of Christ, his resurrection life emerging from the silence and the darkness and the cold of the tomb in the earth. You watched the great candle brought in, and up, and saw its light giving light to the whole place. Actions speak louder than words.

You saw that light descend into the water of the font.

102

It is the light of Christ going down under, beneath the surface of life, into the realm of death, only to be raised in resurrection. When we baptized a few minutes ago those three young children of God, they were symbolically lowered down under, drowned, buried if you like, covered by the waters to die with Christ, only to share his lifting up, his raising.

Who raises? God raises. God raised Christ from the dead. He raises us up as sharers in his Son's resurrection. We are his partners in the enterprise, at his invitation, with his Father's will and wish for us. We have died to the old disfigured humanity. We have been raised with him, and our lives are part of the resurrected life.

It is one of the divine surprises. God often works by surprise. You think you can put your finger on him, and you are wrong. He works by surprise. In the face of all evidence to the contrary, the dead Christ comes from down under filled with an entirely new life whose force blows away the stone from the mouth of the tomb, a force stronger than the gates of hell. It blew the edifice of human history apart, stone set upon stone, for the dark earth was no longer the dead end for humanity, and in the light of this new day all human experience, all human calculation has been knocked sideways and overturned.

And actions will speak louder than words as you come to receive that resurrection life to yourself when you take the body of Christ and his blood, for he comes to you from down under, from beneath the camouflage of bread and wine, in the face of all evidence to the contrary.

He startled the world when under cover of darkness in Bethlehem he suddenly appeared, God with us, here and here to stay. He now appears again, his light suddenly shining from out of earth's darkness, the man from down under, our resurrected Lord, our God, our life!

That Face

What do you do at a time like this? At a time when hopes are dashed, when the world has crumbled into bits, when with friends like this, one scarcely needs enemies. When defeat stalks your street and you have lost the one person who has seemed to make sense of everything in the past, in the present, and for the future, the only thing you can do is to look and remember. You remember the promises. You remember the commitments. You remember the happiness. But you instinctively look for the person you have lost.

There is a mysterious phrase embedded in the Psalms, *and it is God who speaks:*

Seek ye my face: Thy face, Lord, will I seek.

That beloved face, Christ's face, had been taken away by death, had been lost to sight and hidden away forever. It was the end to a promise, the extinguishing of a light in lives that had loved him, had worked with him, had watched him work and had rejoiced at it, and him.

But then something happened to defeat all the wisdom and the experience of humanity: the stone blasted from the sealed mouth of the tomb was the symbol of an explosion of a life-power that was not human but divine as God performed his mighty act and raised Jesus from the dead. The story of Easter, the glory of Easter, concern that face.

104

For Christ's resurrection face was both *un*recognizable immediately *and* recognizable instinctively to the disciples. The ancient prophecy of the Suffering Servant tells us that "his visage is marred more than any man's," and indeed suffering and the death experience are written upon his face — but these marks are now joined with signs of the power of a new and unending life. It is a face transformed, a face suffused with resurrection light, and only the eye of faith can come to terms with it, wants us to look *for* it and to look *at* it.

"Seek ye my face," says the risen Christ. "It is not the face you expect. I have been through hell for you, for love, for love — both love of you and love for my Father, because it was the only way that this could be put right. Well, it *is* put right. And you are made right as a result. I want you to share what is mine, this resurrection experience. It will involve the cross, too, and that is written on my face. And death, too — death to yourselves, your lesser selves.

"My face is different, for resurrection life makes everything different. It took time for my disciples to recognize me; I will wait until you can greet me, knowing me. Meanwhile, seek my face."

And then — and then, "I shall not live till I see God, and when I see him I shall never die" (John Donne).

Christ the Divine Pimpernel

Do you remember this from the story of the Scarlet Pimpernel, the English secret agent in the French Revolution?

> We seek him here, we seek him there,
> These Frenchies seek him everywhere.
> Is he in heaven? Is he in hell?
> The damned, elusive Pimpernel?

He would leave this note behind him, his calling card, before he vanished yet again. You could never catch him. He was always somewhere else, a distance ahead of you. It was not because he was afraid of being caught. He evaded capture in order to do the work he had been assigned.

But not so with Christ, God's secret agent, God in human form. They *had* caught him. He hadn't evaded capture. He was betrayed by one of his own — the sharp businessman of the bunch, Judas. And having caught him, they made an example of him and nailed him to a cross on Skull Place, where he soon died. Then they pulled him down and put him where nobody would want to get at him — sealed in a stone-cold tomb. The end. Life goes on. Dark for some: those who had loved him, who were warmed and lit by the fire of his love, who had followed that light around, who had begun to see things differently in that new light. That light had gone out of their lives. The forces of darkness had had their way.

But had they? Had they? What is this light that reappears? This divine Pimpernel-flicker appearing in the face of all evidence to the contrary? This elusive flame emerging from down under, defying burial, the silence of the tomb, the stillness and cold of death?

This is what we reenact tonight. From the place you would least expect, from dark silence, the light of Christ comes among us, and we catch his light as it is passed from one to another. We see it held high, the great paschal candle. You see, then, the light descend into the water of the font: the light of Christ going down under, beneath the surface of life, into the realm of death — but only to be raised in resurrection. When we baptized a few minutes ago those people and babies, they were symbolically lowered down under, drowned, buried if you like, with Christ in his death, covered by the waters of death, only to share his lifting-up, his raising.

Raised by God, who raised Christ — raised by God as sharers in his Son's resurrection, partners at his invitation and his initiative in the great divine Pimpernel adventure of obeying and completing the Father's will and wish for us: "to be saved by Christ forever!"

Christ's Fight with Fear — to Victory

It is a physical impossibility to stand here looking at you all without a great leap of the heart at what I see. Amid the flowers and the candles, surrounded by stupendous architecture, the air is electric with the atmosphere of faith and joy that this day brings. I have heard you shout. The singing would give our Baptist brothers and sisters a run for their money. I can see your faces and your eyes shine as people's faces do when they encounter the beautiful and the mysterious in any form. Combine what we see with the music we hear, and we have a family of Christians enjoying the work of praising God on this day, the crown of the year. Not for nothing did somebody say to me on Easter Day last year, "Now I'm beginning to understand what a coronation must be like." Call it what you like, but give yourself to the worship and relax into the joy, for "Now is Christ risen from the dead, and become the firstfruits of them that slept" (1 Cor. 15:20, KJV).

Those of you who have been with us this Lent have considered a series of fears that Christians face — the fear of loneliness, the fear of helplessness, the fear of sickness, the fear of old age, the fear of death. We have tried to see how Christ helps us face these fears head-on. He never helps us to evade them or to hope that if we ignore them they will go away. His job is redemption, not administering anesthetics. He knows that people who love him can experience fear.

You heard the account in the Gospel read to you a few minutes ago about three very frightened women. They had put their money together on Saturday night, whatever it was that they could afford — not likely to be much — and when the Sabbath observance was over and the stores reopened for late-night shoppers, they stopped in to buy aromatic oils to anoint the body of Jesus. They knew as they made their way through the dark streets to the garden near the execution site that even the three of them together wouldn't be able to move back that great stone covering the entrance of the tomb. They would need help. But listen, first I want you to hear again the account that Mark wrote. I'm going to read the verses carefully. It pays to give attention to the fine print; the story isn't as simple as it appears.

> When the Sabbath was over, Mary of Magdala, Mary the mother of James, and Salome brought aromatic oils intending to go and anoint him; and very early on the Sunday morning, just after sunrise, they came to the tomb. They were wondering among themselves who would roll away the stone for them from the entrance to the tomb, when they looked up and saw that the stone, huge as it was, had been rolled back already. They went into the tomb, where they saw a youth sitting on the right-hand side, wearing a white robe; and they were dumbfounded. But he said to them, 'Fear nothing; you are looking for Jesus of Nazareth, who was crucified. He has been raised again; he is not here; look, there is the place where they laid him. But go and give this message to his disciples and Peter: "He is going on before you into Galilee; there you will see him, as he told you."' Then they went out and ran away from the tomb, beside themselves with terror. They said nothing to anybody, for they were afraid.

Mark 16:1-8, NEB

And, do you know, *that* is where St. Mark's Gospel

account *really* ends? It ends in terror: "They went out and ran away from the tomb, beside themselves with terror. They said nothing to anybody, for they were afraid." They were not expecting *resurrection*. They were there to pay their last respects to a dead body, hoping they could get access to it to embalm it. They were immersed in their grief. What do you do when you are shattered in bereavement? You keep going mechanically. If you stop, it's all over, you collapse. You find things to do; the momentum helps. But you tend to make hasty judgments because you can't think straight, and you fail to notice things because you can't see straight. Mark tells us that they only noticed the stone moved away when they "looked up." The Greek word really means to recover one's sight — we might say, to do a double-take, to pull oneself together. Then notice that, startled as they must have been, *they still went in*. That took courage. Courage is more than not being frightened. Courage is doing what you have to do despite the fact that you're frightened.

These frightened women were doing *exactly* what two frightened men did with the dead Jesus. Joseph of Arimathea and Nicodemus were both pillars of the religious establishment. They sat on the Sanhedrin, the Council of Seventy who ran the religious affairs of Jerusalem. Both of them had been convinced of Jesus' claims to be the Messiah, but they had hid their conviction for fear of detection by their colleagues, the scandal, the outrage, the ostracism, the banishment, and other punishments they might have to face. But now they went and faced it when they asked Pontius Pilate for permission to take Christ's body from the cross and to place it in the new tomb that Joseph had provided. They knew the cost. They knew the cost to Jesus of their silence during the Council meeting that condemned him to death. They had kept quiet. But now, though they were frightened, they spoke up. They made a declaration. And no doubt they paid the price.

The women go in. The angelic messenger's appearance paralyzes them. He tells them that there has been a resurrection, that they will see Jesus, that they should pass that message to his disciples, and specifically Peter. Peter is in disgrace, but he has to hear the news. There is forgiveness in that message. They flee, "beside themselves with terror," and they disobey: they are terrified and say nothing. Of this Archbishop Michael Ramsey in his wonderful book says, "but silence and fear have their own message. They tell, more than words can, of the overwhelming reality of the Resurrection" (*The Resurrection of Christ,* p. 77).

Fear. Fear all the way around. It is important for us to come to terms with the presence of fear surrounding the death and the early discovery of resurrection. It can, you notice, trigger courage. The women recover their speech and courageously pass the message on — so the other accounts tell us. The disciples are just as terrified. All you have to do is to read Luke's account of Jesus' sudden appearance among them after the Emmaus road incident. They were terrified out of their wits.

Don't for a moment imagine that Jesus did not know what it is to feel fear. His approaching death caused him fear. What we blandly and euphemistically describe as the agony in the Garden of Gethsemane was fear and apprehension in the struggle to achieve his Father's will. It wracked him. But he went on to fight the forces of darkness and death and destruction, the degradation, the suffering, the desolation notwithstanding, knowing as Fr. Thomas Shaw put it so beautifully on Good Friday that it was from the cross that the divine creativity showed itself supremely, for utterly alone, with nothing left to give other than his dying breath, he would draw all people to himself.

The resurrection not only vindicated Christ's promises and the claims of God's love but redeemed the grounds of all fear. His perfect redeeming love casts it out. He brings himself in his life to our lives. If you let him, he will live in you. Now. You may be afraid to let him, but if you can overcome your apprehension and ask him into your life, he will enter it with respect and transfigure it with his life and love. He will help you with your fears not by telling you that they are imaginary but by demonstrating that the sources of those fears can be redeemed. So that if and when fears materialize — as sickness strikes you, injustices crowd in upon you, discrimination wounds you, loneliness overtakes you, helplessness paralyzes you, old age cramps your style, or the approach of that old enemy death hovering in the wings of your life comes front and center on the stage to dominate the scene — he is with you to hold your hand, because your fears are hidden in his wounds. He knows it all. He has been there. And he it is who breathes in you the resurrection words that Paul repeated despite the certainty of his own terrible death:

> I am persuaded, that neither death, nor life, nor angels, nor principalities, nor powers, nor things present, nor things to come, nor height, nor depth, nor any other creature, shall be able to separate us from the love of God, which is in Christ Jesus our Lord.

> Romans 8:38-39, KJV

Christ Alive!

I find myself incapable of standing here looking at you all without a great leap of the heart at what I see. The flowers. The candles. This stupendous architecture. The air, electric with joy and the faith it comes from. The singing which would give our Baptist sisters and brothers a run for their money. The shout which you gave back to me with almost enough power to damage the stained glass. And your faces! I can see your faces and eyes alive as they can be only when they encounter the beautiful and the mysterious in every form, when they are moved by the *mysterium tremendum et fascinans,* the tremble-making and compelling mystery — all this in a setting of worship and choral music as beautiful as we can make it — and we have a family of Christians enjoying the work of praising God on this day, the crown of the year. Not for nothing did somebody say to me on Easter Day a couple of years ago, "Now I'm beginning to understand what a coronation must feel like." Call it what you will, but give yourself to the worship and relax into the joy, for "Now is Christ risen from the dead, and become the firstfruits of them that slept" (1 Cor. 15:20, KJV).

I watched you listening attentively to the Gospel as it was read to you a few minutes ago. Luke is very careful. Every word counts. There are subtleties I want you all to appreciate, and I hope you will forgive me if I read some verses again:

Finding that the stone had been rolled away from the tomb, they went inside; but the body was not to be found. While they stood utterly at a loss, all of a sudden two men in dazzling garments were at their side. They were terrified, and stood with eyes cast down, but the men said, 'Why search among the dead for one who lives?'

Luke 24:2-5, NEB

Note who made the discovery: not the apostles but the women, Mary Magdalene, Joanna the wife of Chuza, who was employed in Herod's household as a most trusted investment counselor, Mary the mother of the apostle James, and some others. Mary Magdalene with her dark and tragic past is a surprising companion to Joanna, a lady of the court; perhaps they were linked with each other by some healing Jesus did. Luke suggests as much earlier in his Gospel (8:3), physician that he was and meticulous about medical detail. These women were petrified with fright at what they experienced, rooted to the ground, paralyzed. The body was gone, the tomb empty. And then the angelic appearance of two men in dazzling garments and their all-important question for the women: Why search among the dead for one who lives?

That question has a challenge in it, a challenge that has still to be faced and answered. Not any longer by these remarkable and brave women whose experience was thought nonsense by the apostles when they told them, but by us, by the church.

The challenge is relevant and contemporary and urgent. It still stings with its demand for an answer. For people are looking for Christ, perhaps without knowing they are looking for him. They are looking for peace, for fulfillment in their lives, for meaning, for a love they have not yet tasted, for answers to questions about themselves to which they have found as yet no satisfying answer. They are looking for truth and depth, they are looking for a home, and they are looking for hope. Christ of the resurrection is their answer. In him all these things lie; they all have their place in him. With St. Augustine it can be said that their hearts are restless 'til they find their rest in Christ.

It is in Christ of the resurrection that the soul can find both home and hope. The challenge to the church is to convey the resurrected Christ to those who seek to find some purpose in their existence — the *resurrected* Christ, not some caricature, some diminished figure nudged out of the resurrection light, practically entombed and effectively dead.

Let me explain. And let me explain in the words of my old father in God, Archbishop Michael Ramsey of Canterbury, who taught me everything and who by the age I was when first I came here in 1972 had already written a marvelous book on the resurrection:

> We are tempted to believe that, although the Resurrection may be the climax of the Gospel, there is yet a Gospel that stands upon its own feet and may be understood and appreciated before we pass on to the Resurrection. *The first disciples did not find it so.* For them the Gospel without the Resurrection was not merely a Gospel without its final chapter; it was not a Gospel at all. Jesus Christ had, it is true, taught and done great things; but he did not allow the disciples to rest in these things. He led them on to paradox, perplexity and darkness; and there he left them. There too they would have remained, had he not been raised from death. But his Resurrection threw its own light backwards upon the death *and* the ministry that went before; it illuminated the paradoxes and disclosed the unity of his words and deeds. . . . It is therefore both historically and theologically necessary to "begin with the Resurrection." For from it, in direct order of historical fact, there came Christian preaching, Christian worship, Christian belief.
>
> A. M. Ramsey,
> *The Resurrection of Christ,* p. 9

115

It would perhaps be comforting to think of Christ as an ethical teacher, a sort of moral guide, a good man who says beautiful things in the Sermon on the Mount, who preaches love and forgiveness, who takes children in his arms to bless them, who feeds the five thousand, who brings joy to grieving souls, who heals the sick — *and that is all true.* The Gospels are full of this sort of unsurpassed teaching and unprecedented goodness. But they have something else, and if you don't have the something else, what you do have is simply not enough. You cannot take the teaching and the example and leave behind the suffering death of Christ and the Resurrection. For in doing so, *you leave him dead.*

It would perhaps be bracing to think of Christ as a revolutionary, a fighter for justice, for human rights — *and that is all true.* He did point out God's preferential option, if you like to call it that, for the poor, the dispossessed, those without anything to give them dignity or hope or a place in the sun. See how he treated women, a revolutionary in his own day and since. It is all true. But leave him there, limit your interest to that, and you limit Christ without his resurrection — *you leave him dead.*

It would perhaps be invigorating to think of Christ as one who smiles on success, who somehow will benefit you materially, make you happy, raise your self-esteem, bolster your self-worth. Some TV evangelists like to think of him that way. They promote a gospel of prosperity, a gospel that makes you feel good about yourself, a gospel of improvement — what a former parishioner, Paul Vitz, calls *selfism* in his wonderful book *Psychology as Religion: The Cult of Self-Worship*. But this is not enough. Such a gospel is criminally deficient without the cross, its sufferings and deprivation, without the obedience of Christ through it all to resurrection, his greatest act of obedience. So deficient is this caricature that *it leaves Christ dead.* Why search among the dead for one who lives?

The challenge to the church — the challenge to you and to me — is to make sure we have the life of the resurrected Christ in us, Christ alive in us, his obedience to the Father's will coursing through our veins so that the ground of our hope, the depth of our love and generosity, the reach of our faith may reflect the light of Christ's resurrected life for seeking souls to discover. And it is ours for the asking if we dare face the price of it. For development in the stature of the fullness of Christ does not come without growing pains, as St. Paul indicated when he wrote in his letter to the Philippians that "all I care for is to know Christ, to experience the power of his resurrection, and to share in his sufferings . . . if only I may finally arrive at the resurrection from the dead" (Phil. 3:10-11, NEB). For when I arrive at the resurrection, to make it my own, "I shall live — yet not I — but it will be Christ who lives in me."

Read My Lips

Promises, promises. We have heard a lot in the past year or so. The politicians have promised us things. Both sides of the Atlantic have been given promises. Mrs. Thatcher, whether you think of her as the Iron Lady or Attila the Hen, has made plenty, and is in a mess over the highly unpopular poll tax that promised equity but has proved punishingly heavy for some who live in areas where the local authorities are big spenders. Here in this country we have read the President's lips about taxes. Enough said. I won't even mention the state of things in the city of New York. And those who make promises are being scrutinized perhaps even more closely than the promises they hold out. Their lives are being looked at to see if behind what they say they have *integrity*. The word means "having it all together" — in this case, in what they say and what they are. It so happens that both the Prime Minister and the President have held up pretty well under the tests for personal integrity. But people have looked, just the same. And others who have made political promises have not passed muster as comfortably.

People break promises all the time. We promise to be on time and we turn up late. Sometimes we don't turn up at all. We purchase something, and when the bill comes due we fail to pay it, even when we know we should pay it. We pledge to the church, and sometimes we miss paying our pledge. Let's not mention paying our income taxes on time. Or paying them at all. We make promises to ourselves. We promise to quit smoking; we keep smoking. We promise to go to bed at a reasonable time; the lights are on half the night. We promise to eat sensibly; we end up in gorging ourselves. We promise to keep our temper; we lose our temper. We promise to write that letter; they're still waiting for that letter. We promise to explain; nobody ever learns why, because the explanation never gets made. For whatever reason, grave or trivial, promises grave and trivial are made and disregarded, ceaselessly, by all of us, to others, to ourselves, to God.

It is part of the human predicament. St. Paul knew all about it. Listen: "The good which I want to do, I fail to do; but what I do is the wrong which is against my will; and if what I do is against my will, clearly it is no longer I who am the agent, but sin that has its lodging in me" (Rom. 7:19-20, NEB).

This continual breaking of promises to our better selves is something Paul finds deeply frustrating. He goes on to say,

> I discover this principle, then: that when I want to do the right, only the wrong is within my reach. In my inmost self I delight in the law of God, but I perceive that there is in my bodily members a different law, fighting against the law that my reason approves, and making me a prisoner. . . . Miserable creature that I am, who is there to rescue me out of this body doomed to death?

> Romans 7:21-24, NEB

Paul says it for us all. The promises he made to himself, the promises he knew he ought to make about himself, those very things we promise to ourselves about ourselves when we are functioning properly, when we have our heads on right and our hearts in tune with our heads

— they get forgotten, abrogated, and broken for reasons of self-indulgence, selfishness, laziness, sloth, lust, greed, envy, gluttony, pride, all the lamentable catalogue of deadly sins. We even make promises never intending to keep them. We do it to ourselves. We do it to each other. We do it to God. It seems on the face of it that, left to ourselves, we are incapable of integrity, of being together in word and deed, in purpose and action.

Have you noticed that this word is on everybody's lips? I have noticed this, here and in Britain. People are questioning the integrity of those who claim spiritual leadership and religious capacities, integrity in the banking community, integrity in the stock market, integrity in the military forces, integrity in the conduct of the law, integrity in the field of medicine. There is real anxiety over the soul of a nation in which integrity seems lacking. It could be that every cart in history has rotten apples in it, and at this stage along the journey the rotten ones have somehow been spotted near the top. It could be that power corrupts, whether it is political power or spiritual power.

Perhaps this preoccupation with integrity in all these quarters will prove to be beneficial. Making ourselves aware that integrity is necessary for the nation's life and acknowledging that we need help from somewhere to get it are two significant steps we can take.

But as you reach to take the nation's pulse, remember this: you have a pulse of your own. You have a heart of your own. If you find that the heart of the nation is no longer sound, perhaps you should turn next to an examination of your own heart. Do not hesitate to ask yourself the searching questions you have been asking of others. Ask yourself, if you will, what you enjoy or what you tolerate seeing on television. Some people spend up to twenty-five percent of their waking hours watching television — *twenty-five percent*. How much goes past you without eliciting any objections? Situations on the soaps where characters break promises of loyalty with each other and the breaking of them is pictured so sympathetically that you find yourself applauding the deceiver, the liar? Violence in all its ugliness, sexual or criminal? Exploitation of the grief of the victims of air disasters and murders and robberies and disease? Alarmist reporting of news incidents? Ruthless and unnecessary prying into the lives of people often already overwhelmed with shame and regret, people who simply want to restore what they have devastated? Talk shows that give the cruel and vindictive opportunity to shout and inflame? Do these things get a reaction out of you? Have you thought about the danger you and I are in as members of a passive society, a society of onlookers, spectators, and voyeurs? Where does integrity fit into that? And that is merely one part of your life to think about in this process of taking the nation's pulse. You might also ask yourself what you do with the money you have left over, if you have any left over. There are many searching questions that need to be answered about your preoccupations — your health, your surroundings, the ecology, street people, your neighborhood, scientific discoveries, history, language, sex, your family and friends — many questions for you to answer as you reach out to take the nation's pulse.

Now, for Christ's promises. You heard in Luke's account in the Acts of the Apostles what Christ said to his disciples as he came to the parting of the ways with them. He promised them that they would receive power when the Holy Spirit came upon them. He instructed them to stay in the city until they were armed with power from above — power to be witnesses to him in Jerusalem and all over Judaea and Samaria and away to the ends of the world, for all nations must hear the proclamation of his death and resurrection, must hear that in him they can find God's forgiveness contingent upon repentance. We read Christ's lips. But we did not hear what Luke adds elsewhere, in his Gospel: that this parting promise made the disciples immensely joyful. They were with him for the final few moments in Bethany, where in the act of blessing them with uplifted hands, he parted from them. He was released from the constraints of geography and time to ascend to his Father. He left nothing of his earthly self behind, because he had given himself in his eternal entirety to us for all time.

It is the greatest paradox that ever could be that he has brought us to where he is, and we are here serving our apprenticeship in this mystery. His presence and his very self are our earthly possession and heavenly destiny. And next week, on the feast of Pentecost, marking the church's reception of the Holy Spirit, we shall celebrate the divine integrity of that promise.

As I Live and Breathe

Always be careful to read the words properly. You may recall that it was only by the greatest stroke of luck that I caught an error in the printing of a parish bulletin, and in my letter which began it. The letter should have said "My dear Parishioners," but in fact it read "My *dead* Parishioners." And would you believe it, a couple of weeks ago, during the upsurge of hostilities between pro-lifers and pro-choicers, I glanced at the Fifth Avenue notice board announcing our liturgies and instead of "Festal Eucharist" the notice read "Fetal Eucharist." There is a lot to be said for checking the print.

Did it register with you what Christ was doing in the last of his recorded appearances with the Apostles, which you heard read as the Gospel for the day? Listen to St. John:

> Jesus repeated, 'Peace be with you!', and said, 'As the Father sent me, so I send you.' Then he breathed on them, saying, 'Receive the Holy Spirit! If you forgive any man's sins, they stand forgiven; if you pronounce them unforgiven, unforgiven they remain.'

> John 20:21-23, NEB

Christ breathed on them. That was the breath of creation. You will remember that that was what the Creator

123

did as the world began. God's breath is the Holy Spirit, the divine life. Christ was doing afresh what his Father did, breathing life, fresh life, *his* life into the nostrils of the people he sent out on his behalf. *His* life — with a newness that can erase the whole of life's blackboard of wrongdoing, rebellion, withholding of love, disobedience, squandering of affection, lack of respect for others, greed, cruelty, anger, jealousy, and whatever else there is that can be written up against an individual who despises God and his requirements for us — his life can wipe the slate clean: the divine forgiveness.

But it is not a sentimental wiping of the slate. It is not a kiss-that-will-make-everything-better sort of forgiveness. It is not as though the things that people do wrong can be dismissed as *mistakes*. Have you noticed how fashionable that term is for wrongdoing? Politicians say they made a mistake when they broke their marriage vows, stole huge amounts of taxpayers' money, lied like fish in the face of all evidence to the contrary. They are generally uncomfortable with the suggestion that they have done something *wrong*. Divine forgiveness doesn't whitewash sin as a mistake. A mistake is when you innocently make a faulty choice. There are two coats. They look alike. In a hurry you grab one, and then you find out later that you grabbed the wrong one. That is a mistake. But when the two coats aren't really that much alike, when you glide by the older and shabbier one and reach for the newer and smarter to claim it as yours henceforth, that isn't a mistake: that is a sin.

You know perfectly well what your wife or husband looks like and what is legitimately permissible between husbands and wives, and when you enjoy doing what is not legitimately permissible with someone else's life partner or anyone else for that matter, that is not a mistake: it is adultery. Nor does forgiveness dismiss it as a mistake. Forgiveness acknowledges the gravity, the harm done, the wreckage caused, the tears of betrayal shed, the shame felt, and says, God's wish and will is that you put this behind you, choose the path of truth and integrity, learn from the hurt given and received, and hope afresh, because God's life can actually erase from the blackboard of the soul the disfigurement and put new marrow into the bones of your endeavor to be your true self, which is what he made you for.

No, the divine life which makes all things new is the breath breathed into our nostrils when we declare our need, our dependency on the forgiveness of a loving Lord for our betrayals of him, not innocent choices faultily made.

> Savior, breathe forgiveness o'er us
> All our weakness thou dost know.

But this breath, this Holy Spirit, goes far beyond the work and activity of forgiveness. It creates *community* when it erases the isolation and fragmented loneliness that sin and self produce. I want if I can to say that more simply. Sin isolates. It creates separation — from God and from God's people. Remove the sin, remove the separation, and community begins. People begin to realize how much others can mean to their lives. Give them a shared commitment, and you can witness what a worshiping community can mean, for instance. You can feel it. This is what Christianity means. You can't be a Christian individual without wanting to be part of the Christian community where you live, where your work takes you, where you find your happiness with your family and friends.

Some of you know my sister, Anne. She was telling me as we finished Easter worship that she now knows what strength a worshiping community can exert upon an individual's life — a palpable energy of a sort she had never known existed. She discovered it here. With you. It was a revelation. She found it life-giving, energizing, renewing. The sheer physical energy she experienced, she said, as the congregation day by day from Palm Sunday through the days of Holy Week to Good Friday and Holy Saturday's shattering climax with the holy noise and the ancient shout of Christ's resurrection carried her on a giant wave into Easter's golden shore, all light and ravishing beauty and rejoicing. She had been borne along, physically, in the community she was part of. That, my friends, is the life-giving breath of Christ's Holy Spirit.

My hope is that she will discover how the worshiping community — you — is energized into extending Christ's new life into the larger community of the poor, the homeless, the dispossessed, the lonely, the inadequate whose lives are reduced and made miserable in this vast city, who exist on a level we could not imagine for ourselves. For the life-giving breath of Christ's Holy Spirit creates not only community but compassion — *his* compassion for individuals — not the patronizing, managing, politically motivated busyness that treats dropouts and losers in our society as units to be moved about on a vast checkerboard, to get them out of nice areas into places where they won't be noticeable as they are being housed and fed, but rather a careful, costly examination of the real reasons that their numbers show no signs of decreasing. Nor is he compassionate merely to those without hope. He also cares for the young who need to be shown heights to which they can aspire, ways to reach the potential they have; he cares for those assisting the development of decent housing projects like the Nehemiah Project in the Bronx and Habitat for Humanity, with which Fr. Kenworthy and some of the parishioners are connected — looking to the future by redeeming the present in costly personal donations of time and physical energy, to help build hopeful lives.

Community, compassion, and *concern*.

The life-giving Spirit of Christ breathes concern for righteousness and truth in the compassionate community. It is a concern free from the interfering, prurient, judgmental attitudes of individuals who have no humility or penitence themselves, and freer still of that awful self-consciousness that rejoices in being "saved" while assuming that others are not. It is the determination of William Blake, who called out,

> Bring me my bow of burning gold!
> Bring me my arrows of desire!

and who vowed not to rest until something was done about the commercial greed that reduced people's lives and dwellings to misery and thralldom. It is the determination of good and brave people like Richard Green, who had a vision for the public education of New York's children.

> Breathe on me, Breath of God,
> *Fill me with life anew,*
> That I may love what thou dost love,
> And do what thou would'st do.
>
> Breathe on me, Breath of God,
> Until my heart is pure.
> Until with thee I will one will,
> To do and to endure.
>
> Breathe on me, Breath of God,
> Till I am wholly thine,
> Till all this earthly part of me
> Glows with thy fire divine.
>
> Breathe on me, Breath of God,
> So shall I never die;
> But live with thee the perfect life
> Of thine eternity.

A Grateful Thanksgiving

When you're driving, it is dangerous to do more than glance in your rearview mirror. What's *approaching* should claim your keenest attention. Lot's wife, if she were here and could speak, would attest to the fact that there are times when it is dangerous to look back. She was urged not to, but she did it anyway, so the old Bible story goes, and she turned into a pillar of salt. Some people indulge in looking back to avoid contemporary challenges and change which they view as a threat. They prefer to live in the past where they feel more comfortable. They resent the onset of years and try to disguise it in every way they can.

But with gratitude and thanksgiving, you *have* to look back. You recall what has been given and done, and love rises to dance in the heart when you remember. We *need* to remember. It's easy to forget, as Christ himself pointed out when only one out of the ten lepers he had healed remembered to go back to thank him. Gratitude is akin to love.

I am far more interested in what a nation feels thankful for than what it takes pride in. It can take pride in a successful revolution against a tyrant or an arrogant ruler. We have seen that. It can take pride in conquests of other countries, or battles, or the spread of a particular influence or language into neighboring peoples or nations. We have seen that. It can take pride in a great architectural monument like the

Taj Mahal. But look to see what nations express thankfulness for: the Armistice in 1918, for example, which marked the end of a struggle in which so many young and promising lives were poured out like water, or the discovery of some great gift to humanity like penicillin or the cure for infantile paralysis, or the signing of the Magna Carta, one of the greatest breakthroughs for individual justice.

But to set aside a day annually to thank God for survival, as this nation does today, is to place a particular mark on a nation's face. And I would suggest to you that a vital component of a nation's spiritual maturity is revealed by what it selects as the object of its gratitude. It says something about this nation's truest and deepest humility — a virtue not frequently evident to other nations in the world — that it thanks God, and thanks him for an insignificant and tiny enterprise begun when twenty women and girls got to work and planned a meal in 1621 — a meal not only for their menfolk but also for any friendly natives of the countryside who would accept their hospitality. The intent was to express the gratitude of that intrepid little community for survival after the horrors of a transatlantic crossing in tiny ships and a year in a strange environment with which they as strangers came to terms only through suffering.

The Thanksgiving meal traditionally involves home and family and friends invited in, and a return to the family unit is in itself often a going back as well as a looking back. And on our way to that family meal we gather for the other family meal, the *eucharist* — a Greek word that itself means "thanksgiving" — in which we look back and remember Christ as he tells us to remember him, in the act of breaking the bread of his body and drinking from the cup of his blood. But when you deal with God, the act of remembering somehow isn't always a matter of looking over your shoulder: you bring Christ into your contemporary life, and because this is so, mysteriously so, you find yourself looking into the future at the same time. When we celebrate the eucharist, we anticipate the heavenly feast and banquet at which we are destined as Christ's friends to be his guests.

Remember Thanksgiving last year? No snow. Apart from that, the year has brought many changes for many people. Who would have thought that the Berlin Wall would be breached? Who could have imagined that Poland and Hungary would have noncommunist governments? Could you have guessed that a hurricane could shatter the cities it did and render so many billions of dollars of damage to life and property? Or that San Francisco would be visited *this* year with an earthquake that killed the people it did? Or that China would massacre its students in a brutal repression of their shout for freedom? Life is very different for many people since we celebrated Thanksgiving last year. Some are finding that they now live on the other side of the world. Things have happened in their lives to bring them joy or anxiety or love or loss and bereavement. Some would find little in their lives to rejoice about with us.

God gives us opportunities each year to be generous at this time to those who need our help. When we bring Christ into our contemporary life, we bring his friends in too — the poor, the shattered ones, the inadequate ones who flood this city, and, God help us all, the forgotten here, those who have lost everything in the great disasters of earthquake and hurricane. Frankly I would choke on my turkey if I hadn't pleaded with you all to respond sacrificially to their needs. I've asked the Vestry to match what you give to send to our Presiding Bishop's Fund for World Relief to help the victims of the earthquake and hurricane Hugo this year. Our people are manning the service staff at St. Paul's Church, where many hundreds of the poor and aged are being given their Thanksgiving dinner today. The cold and the snow increase their need for warm food and Christian care. Your record for generosity is outstanding, as you remember the generosity of Christ's love to them and us, to whom with the Father and the Holy Spirit be ascribed our heartfelt Thanksgiving, praise, and hospitable obedience, here, and hereafter.

Corpus Christi

There are times, as all of us know, when it's wise to quit when you're ahead. Preaching on the same topic can be a case in point. Two years ago, shortly after our much-loved Douglas Webster died — that little canon of St. Paul's Cathedral in London who taught us so much and made so many good friends here — I preached on this very Sunday, the Solemnity of Corpus Christi, about the God who hides himself under bread's disguise and wine's camouflage in the sacrament of the eucharist. Douglas had preached here a remarkable sermon about the God who hides himself, and I quoted him, and I was greatly in his debt to be able to do so. I read the 1986 sermon yesterday very carefully twice, and I honestly don't think I can find a way to preach about this mystery in a way more telling than I was able to do then. But I'll try.

Of the great mysteries about which preachers have become eloquent, the mystery for humankind of the precious body and blood of Christ is among the paramount. I want to begin this sermon by recalling another very good sermon delivered by somebody who had more than a reputation as a good preacher: he had what people have come to realize was a genius for preaching. I commend him and his marvelous books of sermons to you. His name was Austin Farrer and, to look at, he was very forgettable: sandy hair, skinny, bespectacled, and shy. He was an Oxford don with some of the eccentricities alleged to adhere to academics. He was chaplain of Trinity College, Oxford, when first I knew him, with an impressive stack of learned works behind him, some of which he was soon to disown. Then he became warden of my college, Keble, when the great Eric Abbott left to go to Westminster Abbey as dean. But put this man into a pulpit and watch what happened! That *was* unforgettable! His face, the face of a philosopher and theologian, would begin to shine as his words took fire, and the dim candles of our undergraduate souls would be lit with a stronger flame as a result of hearing them. But I don't want to bore you by reminiscing. It is as bad a practice as showing home movies. Suffice it to say that when he preached, the church would fill with his devotees and time would fly on wings. Never was seen a head to turn, never a foot heard to stir. It was magic. No it wasn't: it was God speaking through the heart of a man who loved him, and so the Spirit moved mightily among us. There *is* such a thing as holy exaltation, and sometimes we experienced it. It gave my own religious experience a dimension I've always been grateful for, for he was a bit of a saint as well as a great man, author, thinker, priest, and friend. He loved to talk about God's compassion and the mystery of Christ his Son. We knew he had been close enough to catch a glimpse, and we settled for that. What he had to tell us was *authentic,* marvelous, mysterious, and clear as crystal at one and the same time; it was preaching of the first order, because it had the effect of involving us in what he said and taught.

But there was this one very special occasion, and it was one just such as this; we were getting ready for Christ in his body and in his blood in his sacrament of the altar. He spoke in such a way as to bring us with him to the very brink of the mystery in which we were going to partake in the sacrifice of the eucharist, and he did it by saying something like

133

this: "Through Christ we are to approach God, and so we shall make a better communion if we come with an enlivened idea of the God we are to approach. Let us take this most fundamental point. Let us reflect together on the being of God" (the words are taken from "A Celebration of Faith," p. 184). He went on to liken God's being to a hidden spring from which living waters flow and suggested that getting to him is like swimming upstream in that living water: though the current faces you, you experience no fatigue of spirit as you are drawn to the source and spring. We come to the hidden fissure through which this water flows, the source itself, and, mysteriously, we are permitted into it; gently and carefully it opens its hiddenness to you. And what do you find on the other side? A boundless sea of crystal clearness, full of light and warmth, and you find you have entered the very heart of the Godhead, for

> I come to the place from which the whole lake is filled, where a great cataract of waters flows soundlessly down and spreads without foam, falling from no cliff and issuing from no cavern, but constantly self-supplied as out of nothing, out of a bright clean air.
>
> "A Celebration of Faith," p. 185

These are mystical words, and we were a pack of very ordinary and often ribald and superficial students. But to my dying day, I shall have that picture before me of God's love for us in Christ who gives himself in bread's disguise and wine's camouflage. Camouflage and disguise, indeed, for we are dealing with a God who hides himself in his sacraments, outward and visible signs of an inward and spiritual giving of himself, which is his delight.

The seeds of this sermon were sown on a plane coming home to New York. A pretty young woman student, far prettier than the girls I remember at Oxford, and by no means ordinary, ribald, or superficial, was curled up in a seat behind me and in earnest conversation with a boy who was intelligent, articulate, attractive, and Jewish. Eavesdroppers, we are told, rarely hear good spoken of themselves, and I have no excuse for overhearing their conversation but for the fact that she was answering his questions about Christian doctrine as taught in the Episcopal Church of which she was a member. He knew plenty. He had an interest in these things, and he was asking about this very thing, the sacrament of the eucharist, and what Anglicans believed to happen at it. Her answers left me uncomfortable. Her instruction had been inadequate, her lessons half-baked. As a member of the profession whose responsibility and calling it is to teach the Christian faith as well as an eavesdropper on this conversation, I felt I had heard little good spoken of it.

I was sad because the young woman had apparently failed to receive not only an adequate presentation of doctrine but also the riches of insight, majestic glimpses conveyed to us by wise and holy souls into this mystery of mysteries. They are capable of bringing us much joy and tremendous awe as we stand with them and contemplate that crystal sea of the divine love which communion means we enjoy. For the word *communion* itself means "oneness," being at one with somebody, enjoying somebody and being enjoyed at the same time. There is a mutuality in communion; let us not forget that God is enjoying us enjoying him, the source of all joy, all delight, all happy laughter, all fulfillment. It is at the same time two things: deeply personal, deeply individual, on a one-to-one basis, his enjoyment of us as he takes us to himself, forgives us, helps us to be what he has planned for us to become, to be truly and recognizably his child and to share in some way in his likeness, so that we may say with the psalmist, "but as for me, I shall behold thy presence in righteousness; and when I awake up after thy likeness, I shall be satisfied" (Ps. 17:16, BCP) — it is all this, deeply personal and individual, *and* it is totally corporate, for when we are as close to him as that, we are very near to each other, members of a family, the *plebs sancta Dei,* the holy common people of God.

But what brings this to happen, this unique and dual relationship? What is the catalyst, the agent that brings it into reality? A symbol couldn't. Only another reality could. Christ provides that reality in the eucharist itself. Bread is broken. Wine is poured. In the lovely words of Scripture, Christ makes "himself known in the breaking of the bread." He tells us to do this in order to bring him into our life, which is what he means by "remembering" him. Was ever another command so obeyed? The *plebs sancta Dei* have gathered through dark days and bright throughout the church's history to witness this, to seek this "food of man wayfaring," sinners in hope of forgiveness, sinners who want to see more clearly how they went wrong, where they fell, what can be done to put the wrong right, and knowing that this is the place and this is the food that will sustain them and nourish them for the future and for eternity, for their destiny is in him. They hear his word, his story. They know they come undeserving of so great a gift. They know the gift will be given. They know that little pockets of people the world over have been and are in the same quest for that gift.

That gift is himself. Christ himself says it is his body and his blood:

> In truth, in very truth I tell you, unless you eat the flesh of the Son of Man and drink his blood you can have no life in you. Whoever eats my flesh and drinks my blood possesses eternal life, and I will raise him up on the last day. My flesh is real food; my blood is real drink. Whoever eats my flesh and drinks my blood dwells continually in me and I dwell in him. As the living Father sent me, and I live because of the Father, so he who eats me shall live because of me.

John 6:53-57, NEB

This is no empty symbol, no time-weary remembrance. He comes to us in bread disguised and wine camouflaged as he promised. We receive him, with awe, with stupefaction almost, fully and really present among us. "The Lord is in his holy temple, let all the earth keep silence before him." Do you know this? We sang it in the procession today:

> Word-made-flesh, true bread he maketh
>> By his word his Flesh to be,
> Wine his Blood; when man partaketh,
>> Though his senses fail to see,
> Faith alone, when sight forsaketh,
>> Shows true hearts the mystery.

Risking a Reputation

One of the difficulties about becoming world champion of anything is that sooner if not later you are going to be required to defend your championship. Ask the boxers. Ask the golfers. Talk to Dr. George Guest of St. John's College, Cambridge. He is the doyen of masters of choristers, acknowledged the world over by women and men with choirs like we have here. He told me a year or two ago that the St. Thomas Choir was among the top six in the world. After a giddy spin of elation on my part, depression set in. What in the hell do we do to retain our position? All I can tell you is that we keep trying, and Dr. Hancock's task is to keep that musical treadmill moving not only onward but upward. When you have a reputation, you have a risk.

Today, the Feast of Dedication, when we pray in gratitude "for the fellowship of those who have worshiped in this place" (BCP, p. 204), we look back to those whose generosity and vision provided what we now enjoy — a building in the Gothic style without peer in this nation, a unique choir school endowed and supported with educational standards that match its musical renown, and a history of giving to those in need beyond our doors and often beyond the help of institutions and individuals.

When you have a reputation, you have a risk. Our Lord has many things to say to institutions as well as to individuals. You heard in the Gospel set for today what he has to say about the holiest place in the world to his fellow Jews:

> Jesus then went into the temple and drove out all who were buying and selling in the temple precincts; he upset the tables of the money-changers and the seats of the dealers in pigeons; and said to them, 'Scripture says, "My house shall be called a house of prayer"; but you are making it a robbers' cave.'

> Matthew 21:12-13, NEB

The temple's reputation was that of the dwelling place of God on earth. It was unutterably holy. It was the place of pilgrimage to which devout Jews the world over, from the Diaspora, or Dispersion, would spend a significant part of their lives planning a visit. They sang psalms about it, the Psalms of Ascent, as they are called. They knew there was nothing in the world — no building, no palace — more sacred, more significant. It held in itself and in its beauty the whole nation's sense of itself, its particularity. Such was its reputation, and with it came the risk. Jesus created division and disorder by making havoc among those who benefited financially from the temple's reputation, from the piety of the believers, the devout pilgrims, those with soul-needs who loved their God.

He was saying, "You are bringing this place down to the level of your own profit motive. You are ruining the reputation of this place by bruising the souls of those who want to offer themselves and what they have to God." And he used violence to make them pay attention to the risk to which they were exposing the temple.

What kind of risks do you think we run with our reputation here at St. Thomas? Some are obvious. If you set certain standards for the place — if the floors are so clean you could eat off them, if the choir always comes in on time

139

with white surplices laundered and fresh, if the singing is superb and the liturgy under the vicar's eagle eye is precise, if we try hard to preach truthfully and challengingly and compellingly, if the powerful air conditioning machinery does the job of keeping people fresh and unselfconscious — then there is a sense in which the whole enterprise can be counterproductive: people can and sometimes do assume that we are vastly wealthy and hence that it is sheer hypocrisy for us to speak of additional need. That is the risk you run when an institution has fame and beauty and history and prominence and musical majesty. It is a big risk.

But it is the obvious risk. What are the subtler risks we run when we have a reputation? We run the risk of elitism, of assuming that we know how to do things better, run things better than most other places; that we are a cut above and have something to teach to slower people; that because we know, we attract the elite. This is dangerous, as Paul indicates in his first letter to the church in Corinth, in which he is discussing the inheritance his readers claim and enjoy: "For upon us the fulfilment of the ages has come. If you feel sure that you are standing firm, beware! You may fall" (1 Cor. 10:11-12, NEB). Paul knows the dangers of complacency and presumption. He knows how insidious the risk is to the human soul of superiority and comparing. He had begun this letter on the same theme. He had been told by people in Corinth that there was this elitism among some of them: "Each of you is saying, 'I am Paul's man', or 'I am for Apollos'; 'I follow Cephas', or 'I am Christ's'" (1 Cor. 1:12, NEB).

A second risk you run when you have a reputation is that you might forget the sustained generosity and the struggle to give sacrificially on the part of those who helped establish it. The people whose gifts built and endowed this place so nobly deserve to have their memory honored by efforts equal to theirs. The fact that Grandfather gave a lot doesn't let the grandchildren off the hook. We can't coast along on other people's generosity. You would be surprised at the ease with which we think we can! Again, Paul has something to say to us to bring us up short, to keep us mindful of our responsibility. The church in Galatia evidently needed to hear this as well:

> Make no mistake about this: God is not to be fooled; a man reaps what he sows. . . . So let us never tire of doing good, for if we do not slacken our efforts we shall in due time reap our harvest. Therefore, as opportunity offers, let us work for the good of all, especially members of the household of the faith.
>
> Galatians 6:7, 9-10, NEB

He is only echoing Christ Jesus, who talks about the necessity of giving in order to grow: "Give, and gifts will be given you. Good measure, pressed down, shaken together, and running over, will be poured into your lap; for whatever measure you deal out to others will be dealt to you in return" (Luke 6:38, NEB). Four images of harvested corn: good measure, pressed down, shaken together, and running over. Christ talks about the joy of generosity. This should set us right when our reputation is at risk in a place and parish such as this. For despite what we may think of the *eccentricities,* shall we say, of what our church leaders may decide to say or to do at the national level, the need remains for us to be sensitive to the untold members of the household of faith and support them.

Have you heard about the apostolate one of our priests here pursues with those addicted to alcohol, to drugs, to gambling, to debt, and to overeating, to name some of these areas, and with the children of alcoholic parents as well? Mornings begin early, and much of the work is hidden. But what is not hidden is the enormous energy required to maintain the impressive library of books on sale at the office entrance — the business surrounding this enterprise. It is very busy, very demanding.

Have you heard about Habitat for Humanity, how one of our priests helps with the organization that builds affordable housing? It's a ministry of encouragement, like the work he encourages among the homeless with the Midnight Run, distributing food and blankets through the night. There is need for support, financial and personal, which we must find to give for these works of mercy. And there are many others, such as the Church of the Holy Apostles food program to which we contribute tens of thousands every year. Just ask us. We have to be generous to help educate children in poor areas, to give them a chance to leave New York for the countryside, for camp each summer. We have to help old people do the same, too. We have to help seminaries and individual seminarians from within the parish.

We might be tempted to coast along with our reputation and kid ourselves that there is no need for change, for the discomfort of the possibility of change. But there are risks with our reputation we *have* to take. We have to be looking for new ways to serve Christ with what we have been given. We have to be innovative and courageous. You know as well as I do that the music we make here is a civilizing influence in this chaotic and at times cruel city. We breathe fresh air into its lungs when we make fine music. We are expanding our choral output to three consecutive days midweek — Tuesdays, Wednesdays, and Thursdays. The gentlemen of the choir will be singing Tuesday evensong at 5:30, a midday eucharist the next day at 12:10, and now a Thursday evensong at 5:30. But we need to get this known through the town. This is something we can contribute. It is worship. It is doing something beautiful for God. Will you do two things? Try and support it personally and financially, and get the information to others? I know you're proud of it. Tell people. They will listen. And come yourselves if you can. In this one small but significant and sacrificial way, you will be recognizing the reputation Christians are endowed with. As you heard St. Peter say in the epistle, "You are a chosen race, a royal priesthood, a holy nation, God's own people, that you may declare the wonderful deeds of him who called you out of darkness into his marvelous light" (1 Pet. 2:9, RSV).

The Tattoo Shop

Early last Saturday morning before I went to officiate at a wedding, I found myself with a parishioner on the Portobello Road. Those of you who have been to London know the Portobello Road. It is a Saturday trading place for junk, for genuine antiques, for the rare bargain, and for many more less fortuitous purchases. Stalls and tiny shops by the hundred deal in every imaginable commodity from the past. But one shop I didn't have time to visit: the Tattoo Shop. The window was adorned with photographs of snakes on shoulders, messages of eternal devotion on hands, slinky ladies on chests, foxes on thighs, and many more depictions on many different parts of the human anatomy. I didn't see anybody going in or, perhaps more importantly, coming out with a new design planted somewhere, but I thought for a long time about the quality of permanence of what took place there. Once you'd got it, you'd got it.

That's fine, I suppose, if the Maisie whose name adorns your biceps is the same woman you have lived your life with all the years since as your wife. But what if Maisie got tired of you or you found somebody else? Will the sight of Maisie's name cause you to be regretful or embarrassed or ashamed or will it fuel another's jealousy? I am told that at some expense and after some discomfort, the unfortunate tattoo can be eradicated or concealed. That may be worth the trouble and the expense. But for the most part, once you've got it, you've got it.

Your baptism brought you into existence as a member of God's family. The water poured, the cross made upon your head, the oil of anointing: it was a divine tattoo, permanent, lasting, eternal. It marks you out forever as belonging to Christ. It is as much a part of you as anything could be. Deeper than the Portobello tattoo, which is only skin deep. *This* tattoo is eternal: a soul tattoo. You can ignore it. You can cover it up. You can be sick of the fact that it is there. You can pretend you never have had it. You can indeed forswear it, abandon it, deny it in what you think or in what you do. Your present lifestyle may call it into question and even into disrepute. But it is there. It is a part of you. It may cause jealousy. It may embarrass you. It may cause misunderstanding. It may in fact impede you if you own up to its presence in your life. But it is there. You carry its mark through this world and into the next. Once you've got it, you've got it.

This is the day when as a large parish family we meet in our worship to consider our heritage — who and whose and for whom we are. It is Dedication Sunday, our Feast of Dedication. We come to pledge ourselves again at several levels, as family members of Christ, bearing the divine tattoo of our common baptism, belonging to him, responsible to him, responsible for our representation of him to the hordes who pass up and down Fifth Avenue past our front doors. We are the inheritors and the beneficiaries of so much. We know, and we should know, who we are, whose we are, and for whom we are.

Because of this we must ask ourselves a question. I suppose it's healthy to keep asking yourself questions. I find myself asking the same question: what is St. Thomas Fifth Avenue supposed to be doing here? What is it supposed to be saying not only to the patient and loyal crowds who come week by week to offer themselves, their souls and bodies, in worship and penitence and hope to God in Christ and to work with each other for others in between times, but what is it supposed to be saying to the hundreds of thousands who pass this building every day? To the rich and busy? To the thoughtful and learned? To the hopeful and the intelligent? To the unsuccessful and disappointed? To the poor and forgotten? To the inadequates, the unbalanced, the hostile, and the idle? What is this place supposed to be doing here? We take up a lot of space. We are near such important institutions as the Museum of Modern Art. We open at seven and close at six. We offer warmth in the winter and shadowed cool in the heat. For large parts of our day there is no mass activity going on; there are hours of silence, and there are times when the organ speaks. People use it to pray in, to sit still and to contemplate in, to find rest in, to talk quietly in, to read both the Bible and their books and newspapers in. They use it as a retreat from the noise, as a place to calm their jangled nerves after some unpleasant encounter or other. They use it to cry in, without drawing attention to themselves outside. People pour their grief out here. I have seen it many times. They use it as a place to pull themselves together, to summon the courage for the next interview, whether it's a doctor or a banker or a prospective employer. They use it like this because they know they can be both alone and in a friendly place where there is space to think and there are beautiful things to see. They use it as a shrine, a place where God is loved and worshiped in the beauty of holiness.

Of all the thousands who come in and out, for good reason or for little reason except that they know they can rely on the welcome of this lovely place, only a fraction can or do remain to worship with the parish family. And outside there still remain the millions who pass this place, looking for something else, going somewhere else, their lives and their hopes fixed on somebody other than Christ perhaps.

I know what we *seem* to be. We seem to be a sort of Gothic success story, with a superb building and superb music, with a famous choir of men and boys who walk correctly on carefully polished tile floors as they sing, their surplices clean, and their ruffs where they should be (for the most part). We seem to be well-heeled, well-staffed, well looked after. True, compared with the 666 Building beside us and the Museum Tower behind us we are dwarfed in a way that our architects might never have contemplated. True, we have no lawn, no trees in a close, no car park or floodlighting. But we have a strategic location unparalleled in the Anglican world. We are in the very thick of everything. So what are we supposed to be doing?

Very possibly, four things. I submit to you that we are here to suggest, to remind, to invite, and to inspire.

For good or ill, we have taken our place among the riches of the world, the financially and economically powerful of the world, the top jewelers of the world, one of the foremost modern art collections in the world, to suggest that over mankind's creativity and grandest achievements and over superlative technical skills and the expressions of the artistic soul of humanity arches the judgment of God. Calmly and without ostentation, Christ on his cross looks down on Fifth Avenue from above our main great doors, his eyes surveying the glory of all that inventive and successful evidence of human possession. Beneath his feet the words in great letters: "*Thou* Art the King of Glory O Christ."

All you need to do is to lift your eyes. Much lower than the skyscrapers and seemingly insignificant among the soaring buildings stands this suggestion to one of the busiest streets in New York, that there is another dimension to this world that has to be accounted for: the power of the love of God. The arms of Christ are outstretched, for us, in welcome.

The suggestion is given in the outstretched arms, in the open eyes, and in the words of homage from the *Te Deum*

147

that triumph and failure, joy and pain, victory and death are not as widely spaced as some would like to think, that such things as suffering, betrayal, and human weakness are as much involved in the glory of Christ's sovereignty as success and power and "arriving" on Fifth Avenue. This suggestion of a wider dimension is emphasized in Christ's arms outstretched to embrace *every* fortune in the human endeavor, that

> Neither death, nor life, nor angels, nor principalities, nor powers, nor things present, nor things to come, nor height, nor depth, nor anything else in all creation, will be able to separate us from the love of God in Christ Jesus our Lord.

> Romans 8:38-39, RSV

Second, this place is here to *remind*. There is not one of us in the Christian family who does not need the memory jogged on occasion about who we are and whose we are. We have a heritage to acknowledge, a relationship to live up to. St. Peter makes this point with force in his first letter: "You are a chosen race, a royal priesthood, a dedicated nation, and a people claimed by God for his own, to proclaim the triumphs of him who has called you out of darkness into his marvellous light" (1 Pet. 2:9, NEB). If any of us as Christians has an identity crisis, that is all we need to know. The heritage is noble. It is clearly stated: we are a chosen race, a royal priesthood, a dedicated nation, a people singled out with a vocation, with a proclamation to make, not an admission to be wrung out of us. We are called to make this proclamation as members of a priesthood, and a royal priesthood at that, a priesthood of which sacrificial service and lifelong loyalty to people are integral parts. This priesthood calls for more than individual responsibility; it entails a corporate awareness, a family membership, and today's celebration of the feast of our dedication to St.

Thomas is designed to emphasize it. We are not subscribers to a philosophy; we bear a divine tattoo, a family responsibility to people beyond our ranks, to bring God to them and to bring them to God with us.

And so the third task that we are here to perform is to *invite*. We need to evangelize, to attract and to convince people by the heritage we possess to join us. We need to uplift Christ so that people may long to know more about him, to know him and to love him, to love him and to serve him, to serve him and to live for him, to share our destiny in him.

Mere words recited won't achieve this. They never do. I am probably more wicked than most of you in feeling quite unmoved by men shouting at me on Fifth Avenue that my sins which are many can be washed away; the flailing arms and the Bible raised and haranguing tones do little for me. But a welcome, a smile can work wonders for me in a place like this when I come in to worship, to see what the worship is like. And a place like this must not only look beautiful, it must *be* beautiful in its reassurance to the new and shy and lonely that they will be welcome and that they are wanted. They have a right to know that this place is prayed in. I am convinced that if we persist in our struggle to get the worship right, so that the atmosphere of this superb place rings with the worshipful love of Christ and resounds with concern and patience and joy, then it will be the vessel for all our activities for others in this city and beyond its bounds that proclaim Christ's kingship over us. Souls will feel *invited* to belong to the Christian family of forgiven sinners.

Invited, then *inspired*. Inspired not merely by this wondrous place and what goes on officially in it but by what it has always stood for: sacrificial generosity. Think how we began: with a stupendous, reckless, loving, and courageous act of generosity to the victims of the 1906 San Francisco earthquake, when all our reconstruction funds were telegraphed to the West Coast and we had to begin entirely again. Begun — and continuing. The need to give did not stop after the money poured in to build this glorious place. The need is with us still, for God's work still has to be accomplished, and still we need to give seriously, sacrificially, steadfastly. It is when we are giving more than we thought we ever could, more than we think we ever should, that our heritage mysteriously displays its integrity; for an ungenerous Christian is a contradiction in terms. When we commit ourselves to this hard road, we are doing no more than following in the steps of the one whose divine tattoo we bear, who gave of himself to the point of shedding his most precious blood for us and our salvation. This costly self-giving spirit of his, unselfconsciously seen in us, is what will inspire, for it is the real thing, the authentic ingredient in the life of a Christian community and in the soul of a Christian individual.

The sign of the cross in baptism which we wear is the symbol of the generosity of a God who "so loved the world, that he gave his only begotten Son, that whosoever believeth in him should not perish, but have everlasting life" (John 3:16, KJV). Our tattoo: and we can thank Christ that if we've got it, we've got it!

Our P's and Q's — Thanksgiving

A friend was describing an experience in the revolving doors of Bloomingdale's recently. He allowed a brisk young woman to take his place; without a word she took it and whirled through. He called out to her, "Excuse me, did you say something?" She turned and said, "No!" He replied, "I thought I heard you say 'thank you.'" Most of us learned to mind our p's and q's when we were small. When people forget, it can make life bleak.

Of all the things that the nations of the earth set store by, thankfulness does not rank very high. It is most unusual for a nation to be known and set apart as a *grateful* nation, a nation that says "thank you," that makes an act of Thanksgiving a principal national celebration. People like to celebrate the anniversary of a revolution that freed them — look at France, look at Russia — or the ending of a war, or the fall of a tyrant, or the triumph of a hero, historic or mythical, or a feast with roots in pagan times. But to celebrate *gratitude* is extraordinary and, I think, laudable. It takes us out of ourselves, our achievements, our accomplishments, our national characteristics. We say thank *you:* we look beyond ourselves to somebody else.

"Not unto us, O Lord, not unto us, but unto *thy* name do we give the praise" — somebody else: our God, our Deliverer, our Sustainer, our Maker, our Redeemer, who loves and cares for us and, as Christ so movingly tells us, knows every hair on the crowns of our heads. Somebody, in fact, immeasurably greater than we are, compared with whom all our human celebrated achievements, our victories and successes, our historic excuses for any sort of human excesses, pale into selfish insignificance. And that that emphasis on the One we thank prevents our celebration, thank heaven, from tumbling into national complacency, jingoism, or chauvinism.

How could a bedraggled bunch of people reduced and battered by the miserably cold winter of 1620, in a territory unfamiliar and inhospitable, have recovered their spirits sufficiently to press on, to plant and grow and harvest and then plan a meal of thanksgiving for a hundred, unless they were relying on the grace of faith in a loving Deliverer, Sustainer, Maker, and Redeemer? He had brought them through a frightful ordeal. For their survival they turned not to self-congratulation or careless relief, but to him, and then to others beyond their gates whom they welcomed to share what they had. They forgot themselves for a space, their bereavements, their fears for the future, the vagaries of climate and native hostility that loomed before them. They forgot the resurgence among themselves of evidences of the old Adam they had discerned and disowned in their religious oppressors back in England: intolerance, narrow-mindedness, spite cloaked in spirituality. They forgot themselves and they remembered instead their p's and q's. To God. To God.

We do what we can to remember those who are not able to celebrate this day as they would like: the hostages still in Iran and Beirut, all American prisoners of conscience, their families, and those who have no one to remember them. The old, the poor, the improvident, the inadequate, those who starve quietly, those forgotten multitudes that like the saints "no man can number," God's special friends. The

Christian thing is to mind our p's and q's. Over forty of us will go to St. Paul's — some are already there — to serve and help with the dinner for some seven hundred of these poor people. You can mind your p's and q's in a special way by giving heavily to the men who will come among us in a few moments. Your gifts will be sent, all of them, to our Presiding Bishop's Fund for World Relief of famine and the starving.

And we do this here in a setting of thanksgiving — which is what the Greek word *eucharist* actually means. We look back in thanksgiving to Christ our Savior. We bring him here with us under the disguise of bread and wine. We take him with us to our celebrations today. We look forward in gratitude as he lives on in us, anticipating the heavenly banquet we are destined to attend as Christ's friends to be his guests, Christ who has loved us always, saved us, our Lord, "the same yesterday, today, and forever."

Creatures of Habit

There are some customs we can wave a not-so-fond farewell to, like corporal punishment in schools. I can attest to the embarrassment of that experience. I was once caught looking over my shoulder into a tall mirror at the criss-cross marks on my rear, received for some infraction of a school rule, and my father, who had seen the reflection through the open door of my bedroom, was scant in his sympathy. Or hazing, which is often demeaning, sometimes humiliating, perhaps painful, and occasionally dangerous, as we all know. There are some customs we can tolerate. I happen not to mind the parting benediction "Have a good day." I like opening the door for a woman. I like good manners.

People *need* customs. They are a primitive, tribal assertion of identity, of reminding yourself as well as others who you are and whose you are. *What* these customs refer to, and above all, *whom* they refer to, helps us to gauge the rate and the path of progress into what we call civilization. Some people, many people here in church, would declare the death penalty a barbaric custom; others, equally knowledgeable and no less forgiving, could find it in their hearts to defend it. There are holy customs, customs hallowed by their origins and sanctified in their observance through the passing of the years. Read the Old Testament and you will find on page after page a developing structure of customs for holy eating, holy living, holy law-making, holy life-making. Much of it is based on common sense, on the practical recognition of what the times were calling for. There are stories of mountains and rocks and walls and wells that people used to remind themselves about the living wisdom of our God, their place in his plan, and his place in their plan. It was a two-way street down which they could travel, and they did. For customs set people apart, often physically, as in the case of circumcision.

We are inheritors of a *Christian tradition*. The patterns of our worship may change, but the components of worship are customs like pearls of great price, and while some may bore us, others are deeply significant. We hand our customs on every time I reach into the font for water to baptize.

Deeply Christian and deeply idiosyncratic also is the custom of registering gratitude to God. From earliest days, holy people had a round of thanksgiving celebrations for food to live by and safety to live in. You heard the last verse of the Old Testament lesson: "And you shall eat and be full, and you shall bless the LORD your God for the good land he has given you" (Deut. 8:10, RSV). The church has taken this on, and this country has made a principal observation of it, and here we are today to observe it.

"I will thank thee, O LORD, with an unfeigned heart" we say in the Psalms. The festival we celebrate is for survival, a remembrance of the time in 1621 when twenty resourceful women got to work and cooked dinner for a hundred in honor of God's generosity and mercy. A disingenuous act now recognized to be of sheer genius began a custom that has dignified this nation *and consecrated it,* no less, to the Lord and Giver of all life who protects all life and in so doing begets hope in the face of all evidence to the contrary. But the custom of Thanksgiving began as an act of hospitality to people who didn't belong by blood or belief to

155

the little group of survivors. It was not an act of self-congratulation. It was not an act of chauvinistic accomplishment. It was not a proud remembrance of battles won or tyrants slain. It was an expression of loving-kindness by people who themselves could sing of the loving-kindness of the Lord. *That* is what makes this day so holy and so strong to set its seal on the heart of a nation. And I'm sure you would agree with me that we must never lose sight of its genius and origins.

> For what great nation is there that has a god so near to it as the LORD our God is to us, whenever we call upon him? . . . Only take heed, and keep your soul diligently, lest you forget the things which your eyes have seen, and lest they depart from your heart all the days of your life; make them known to your children and your children's children.
>
> Deuteronomy 4:7, 9

For this reason many people still need to be given that hope here in this country, and our duty as inheritors of this custom is to maintain that hope.

There are many in this city at this moment who have little hope of a full stomach or the tenderness of a family's ties or laughter or enjoyment of this feast today. The old, the poor, the inadequate, and God help us all, the *forgotten* are around us as I say these words. Some there are who will be fed today, thanks to your generosity and your service in St. Paul's in the Chelsea area, where some of our clergy will soon be.

Each year we give what we get from you today to the Presiding Bishop's Fund for World Relief. You have had a record of outstanding generosity in the years you have supported this. Do you remember my telling you of the dying Ethiopian child, starving, in the last days of his misery? You poured funds into the cause that year. Your realization of this unique custom of thanksgiving will suggest to you how generous you should continue to be as we give thanks to God in this eucharist, as we take this custom into the dimension of the sacrament. For we remember his lovingkindnesses, "which have been ever of old" as the psalm says, in order to look forward to that eternal thanksgiving when with those we have loved long since and lost awhile we shall be Christ's guests, who loved us then and loves us now, and to whom with the Father and the Spirit be our heartfelt thanksgiving, praise, and hospitable obedience, here and hereafter.

The Opening Door

Dedicated to the Choristers Who Graduated
from the St. Thomas Choir School

When in Rome, do as the Romans do, we are told. Good advice. Romans like a long lunch. Preferably with wine. On the last day of my stay with our old friend Monsignor Jean Louis Tauran, who works for the Cardinal Secretary of State in the Vatican, we did what the Romans do: Bishop Michael Marshall and I enjoyed a long lunch with Monsignor Tauran. Then he took us into ancient Rome. We saw the oldest churches. We saw Roman antiquities. And then, in the last church we looked at, St. Sabina's Basilica, I saw something I will never forget: the marble side of an ancient Roman coffin, on which was carved in bas-relief a large double door. One of the doors was half open — or, as the ancient pagan Romans saw it, on its way to closing. Life was over. The doors to life were to be shut and locked. It was poignant.

But it was a parable. At least to a Christian it was a parable. To a Christian the door of life was opening. And beyond the door?

This is a Sunday on which, as most of you can well imagine, it is both a joy and a difficulty to preach. For in front of me sit young men whose time with us is over. In my study I have the photographs of every class that has graduated since I came here in 1972. This class is the seven-

158

teenth. Space is running out upstairs, and we shall have to double up next year. I, with others, have shared the pleasure of their company and in some cases the privilege of their friendship, and watching them leave us is hard. I have witnessed their growth and the development of their personalities, their humor, as well as their ability to sing gloriously and to lead us in worship. Now I am going to address them principally and primarily, and the rest of you can regard yourselves as amiable eavesdroppers.

I can guess a little, at what you may be thinking. A door is opening for you, and you have to go through it. You can't stop where you are, even if part of you wants to. You may have enjoyed your years at the Choir School. I hope you have. There's not another school building like it, and very few to touch it for sheer *niceness*. All a school needs, you pretty much have at 202 West 58th Street. Except for a swimming pool. Give me time. Until Stephen Garcia makes his first million and gives you one, we could try flooding the gymnasium to a depth of five feet if you like and let swimmers and basketball players fight it out as to whether it stays that way. But seriously, you have received from the headmaster and Dr. Hancock and all the other people there at the school all the care and the encouragement you needed and deserved.

But the door is opening, and you start to go through it today. I want to suggest to you that it is a door of hope, a door of opportunity to grow, a door of joy. Why? I'll tell you why. Christ claims that *he* is the door; John in his Gospel records Christ as saying so. "I am the door" (John 10:9, RSV). Through Christ, people find access to God. "Through him," says St. Paul, "we . . . have access to the Father" (Eph. 2:18, NEB). Jesus opens the way to God. You heard him say in the Gospel for today, "No one knows the Father except the Son" (Matthew 11:27, RSV). The writer of the letter to the Hebrews says that Christ is "the new and living way" (Heb. 10:20,

159

RSV) by which we can go in and come out boldly and without fear. That very phrase was precious to people of Jesus' time. The freedom to go in and out without fear was essential to a life of security and total safety.

With Christ the door you will be safe. You can be certain of three things. You can be certain that if you say you're sorry for not having pleased him, for not having lived up to what you know he wants you to be and to become, if you apologize to him, turn back to him, tell him you love him despite what you have done and failed to do, there will be swift and deep forgiveness and the strength to go on and become what he has in mind for you.

You can be certain that your prayers will be answered if you pray through Jesus Christ. He promises that. "Ask anything in my name . . . and it will be given to you" (Matt. 7:7-8). It won't necessarily be the way you want, but if you place the matter in his hands, you can be certain that he will do what he promises and intercede on your behalf. And then you can thank him.

You can be certain that if in his name you are generous, that generosity will be met by him and the floodgates of the divine generosity will be opened to you. Listen to him; it's magnificent:

> Give to everyone who asks you; when a man takes what is yours, do not demand it back. . . . If you love only those who love you, what credit is that to you? Even sinners love those who love them. . . . And if you lend only where you expect to be repaid, what credit is that to you? Even sinners lend to each other to be repaid in full. But you must love your enemies and do good; and lend without expecting any return; and you will have a rich reward: you will be sons of the Most High, because he is kind to the ungrateful. . . . Give, and gifts will be given you. Good measure, pressed down, shaken together, and running over, will be poured into your lap.

Luke 6:30-38, NEB

These three things you can count on with Christ the door: penitence, prayer, and generosity. That security is *the door of hope.*

Second, it is in Christ that there is opportunity for growth. You can't pull yourself up by your own bootstraps. Distrust these silly little books of self-improvement advice. They don't really work. And frankly they're superficial. Someone has described the English as a nation of self-made men who worship their creator. St. Paul has something better to offer: the hope we have "to grow into the measure of the stature of the fullness of Christ." One way to ensure such growth is to stick close to him in the sacramental life. I have watched you Sunday by Sunday coming to receive the body and blood of Christ in the sacrament of the altar at the eucharist. His life is living in you. Keep coming to receive him. Keep the relationship fresh and strong. Keep on coming even if you should find it inconvenient or a bore, even when you know that because of something you've done you are more than usually unworthy to receive him. Just tell him you're unworthy and unready and feel hopeless and rebellious and even sick of the whole business — *and still come.* You will grow little by little despite yourself into the measure of the stature of the fullness of Christ.

Third, Christ is the door of joy. He wants you to share his joy, that yours might be complete. It is part of his plan for you to discover his joy in your life. You will discover it in endeavors earnestly undertaken, in tests honestly taken, in challenges physical as well as spiritual faced squarely and cleanly conquered. You will discover it when you fall in love and are loved in return. That sort of joy is heady stuff; it makes the world go round, and it may make you a little dizzy. But my hope is that you will discover this marvelous joy, for there is something of Christ's joy in it. And just as God enjoyed his creativity when he looked upon it, "and behold, it was very good," you will discover joy as you exploit your creativity, as you make music or listen to it, as you and your loved one start to build a life together. You will discover it in winning, and you *can* discover it in losing. You will find that there is joy to be discovered in sickness and failure and pain as well. You will discover it in laughter and the love of friends, and you *can* discover it in solitude and silence. It is there for the asking, because Christ is *here* for the asking, and where he is, there is his joy. He wants you to have it, so that yours may be full.

Christ the door. We are told in Scripture by Christ himself that the door is "narrow." This doesn't mean that Christ is difficult to deal with, awkward to get by, hard to negotiate. It means that he asks a lot of you. He expects a lot from you. His standards have to be grown into, because where he walks it is often hard walking. It is called the *via crucis,* the way of the cross, and you are expected to carry one daily. But then he tells us today to learn from him, to take his yoke, for his yoke is easy and his burden is light.

The door is opening wider now. Soon you will be through the door of Choir School life and looking at life beyond. We are glad to have brought you to this moment, glad to have been with you on your journey so far, and I commend you, with all this great parish family who love you so and want such great things for you, into God's care, for time and for eternity.

Tackling the Big Wall with a Tiny Hammer

O f all the pictures that have come to us during this past momentous week of the breaching of the wall between Western and Eastern Germany, the one that spoke to me most profoundly was not, surprisingly, that of all the young people standing and dancing and singing on top of it, nor of the hordes pouring through the permitted gaps in it, nor of the East German guard proffering a flower to a young woman from the West side sitting on it, but that of a young fellow with a totally inadequate hammer and chisel chipping away at it. It was the parable of the wall. With resources utterly unequal to the task, with strength completely ill-matched to the steel and concrete that compose it, he nevertheless tackled the unyielding and inhospitable surface and succeeded in scarring it, punishing it for having so cruelly divided a nation and causing so many tears and separations. The parable of the wall: the determination in the face of all evidence to the contrary to contribute some-thing significant despite the poverty of the offering. This is what faith does. This is how it can express itself. Reckless, perhaps. Determined, certainly. But motivated by a vision that neither poverty nor inadequacy can quench.

You heard the two stories of widows in this morning's lessons. With resources utterly unequal to their tasks, they nevertheless expressed their faith. Elijah asked a poor widow collecting sticks for her pitiful fire to bring him some water and a piece of freshly baked bread. Christ watches in the Court of the Women in the temple in Jerusalem as a poor widow gives two *lepta,* the tiniest coins minted, known as the thin ones.

The point is that they had nothing whatever of value left to give, but they gave what they needed to sustain their own lives to God, to God's representatives. A handful of meal, a drop of olive oil, and a couple of sticks were all she had to keep her and her son from starving. The last meal for a starving woman. Another hungry woman went into the temple as Christ sat opposite the treasury watching the crowds pouring in to pay their dues. The rich put in their large amounts. And then there was this poor widow who put in "two mites which make a farthing." You will remember Christ putting a cost on two sparrows — "Are not two sparrows sold for a farthing?" So what she contributes would just about pay for two tiny, insignificant, virtually worthless birds, useless in the world's eyes as offerings. The Greek word for a mite was a *lepton,* "a thin one," as I said, the most minute of any coinage minted. It was all she had. But her faith brought her to give the last of it.

Examine this faith. Can yours compare with it? A faith that drives you to be generous with the last thing you've got? When you have nothing more to give, to part with the last fistful of meal, the last drop of olive oil, the last couple of sticks, the last penny? What sort of faith would make you look starvation in the face, death's door, and still give? What sort of faith would make you attack the Berlin Wall with nothing more than a tiny hammer?

In the first place, I would suggest, it is a *faith of gratitude.* The heart that is filled with this sort of faith is convinced beyond all doubt of the generosity of a loving God. There is no fear that somehow this generosity will dry up, that the lifeline will be snatched away. Experience has taught that soul that just as God's mercies are new every morning, so are his generosities. So there is little fear of failure. This attitude is not only unstoppable but infectious, and quite unselfconsciously so. A man you and I have heard of — it happens that he was a priest — had a church he was proud of and a parish he loved. His church was burned down. Together he and his people raised the money to put it back to what it had been. They were still collecting for the restoration and worshiping in a temporary wooden building when San Francisco nearly disappeared in the 1906 earthquake and fire. The following day he gathered his vestry around him and asked the treasurer what the restoration fund stood at. One million two. Worth over thirty million in this day and age. He turned and said, "There are five dollars in the fund. I telegraphed one million two hundred odd thousand to the victims of the earthquake this morning. Their need is far greater than ever ours could be." All he had left was a handful of meal, a drop of oil, a couple of sticks, and there was a church to be built: *that* was the loaf he had to make. Most of you know the story: within ten days one million four had been thrown into the kitty; the great city had responded with an explosion of generosity. Money kept coming. People wanted to help. The plans changed. What was called for was not a restoration of the old but rather something new. A glorious design from the finest architect. And you are sitting in it. It is the story of this place. It is the testament of a faith of gratitude, convinced beyond all doubt of the generosity of a loving God. If those of you who are visitors or otherwise new to this place are wondering about the curious atmosphere of joy and freedom combined with an awe and reverence here, that beginning again with nothing in that priest's hands is the secret of it.

For God did a new thing, as he had promised of old. He always has a new thing to give to you, but he can do so only when your hands aren't full, clutching something else to yourself. You may find that you will have to surrender what you most hold dear, something you are convinced is vital to your life and survival, before you will be ready to receive the gift he has to make your life fuller.

The name of the theologian Herbert Haag is not familiar to me, but he writes with real grace about this:

> God punctuates our lives with painful crises that, for that moment, seem to be the end of everything. . . . But when God takes something away from us, he does so only to give us something better in its place, to make us ready for a new task or mission that he has in store for us. God likes to leave us with empty hands so that he can fill them again for us. Whenever we think the end has come, that is just the time when we are due to make a fresh start.

The people of St. Thomas Fifth Avenue could add a hearty Amen to that. And isn't this exactly what the Christian life is all about? A new start? A fresh beginning, a constant discovery of some new thing to which God may be calling us when our hands are free to grasp the opportunity, to seize the day, and "on Occasion's forelock watchful wait," as John Milton says in *Paradise Regained*.

So I suppose that if it was a *faith of gratitude* that made the widows do what they did in the two stories we heard, it was also a *faith of readiness* that allowed them to respond in the way they did, with reckless generosity of heart. All our nations' leaders this weekend have some brave decisions and tough challenges to their generosity to face with situations taken out of their hands by a spontaneous and sacrificial explosion of a taste for freedom. A nation of people has decided to take its future into its own hands, to wrest it from the hands of those who would control them *and* from the hands of those like us who form the balance of power. The situation of the East German people is something new. God is doing a new thing, and we are witnessing it. How we help with our attitude and our prudence in balancing rightful self-interest with the desire to be of real service to a nation newly in turmoil will determine the quality of both our faith of gratitude and our faith of readiness. Remember and pray for that youngster chipping at the Berlin Wall with a totally inadequate tool, and thank a loving and generous God with the readiness of your lives to be responsive to divine surprises. Be grateful! Get ready! Can you echo the great words of Holy Writ, "The Lord hath given: the Lord taketh away. Blessed be the name of the Lord"?

The Test

If I tell you that I am mightily pleased to be among you, you can guess what I mean. As much as anything else, this involuntary separation from you has been a test for me. Speaking of tests, St. Paul says it for all of us in his letter to the Romans:

> let us even exult in our present sufferings, because we know that suffering trains us to endure, and endurance brings proof that we have stood the test, and this proof is the ground of hope. Such a hope is no mockery, because God's love has flooded our inmost heart through the Holy Spirit he has given us.

Romans 5:3-5, NEB

There. Inescapably we find a counter to any temptation to indulge in self-pity. God's love, Christ himself, is there where we hurt and when we suffer loss, right inside the experience of suffering — *not* outside it or outside us when we go through it.

Only with this in mind is it worth my saying anything to you at all, and I wanted to say it to you as soon as I physically could. Briefly, and once only.

Since I last saw you all there has been what you may describe as some *turbulence* in my life: nothing of ultimate significance, but enough to alter my landscape temporarily.

For a time I am, like the centurion in Matthew's Gospel, "a man under authority" (Matt. 8:9) with certain initiatives no longer presently mine to take. I am content to sit back and be ministered to, to watch approvingly and gratefully as things are done for God and for his people, and to benefit from the loving care and concern first of doctors and surgeons and nurses with their astonishing skills, and then of my colleagues and parish family and friends which have come my way in a flood since my encounter just about three weeks ago. These medical people know already how indebted I am to them for their brilliance in bringing me to this day and hour. My own cherished physician is a parishioner and is here today.

But I could not leave this point without a word about two more people in particular: my principal colleague, your vicar, Fr. Fertig, whose tireless competence and large heart have embraced the task of conveying the news to the parish family, monitoring and reporting the progress, maintaining the standards of worship that he knows I set for myself and all of you, keeping this great Gothic ship on an even keel, and inspiring you all to keep the faith and to help me with your prayers.

The other person is my beloved Anne, my sister, whom more and more of you have come to know. She has the patience of an angel. Perhaps with her fizzy brother she requires it. But her cheerful care and her disposition are becoming known to people in the parish, and she is an example to me.

And how can I begin to thank my colleagues and family in this wonderful parish and city? For their gentleness. Their generosity. The flowers. The food. (And, let it be said, the spiritual comfort which comes in bottles.)

There were occasions for much laughter in hospital, not least over the garment I was required to wear, which came to my knees and was backless: I referred to this necessary but unaesthetic gown as my *dress*, a continuing embarrassment to me and to my sister, who was forever trying to hide my nakedness. I was reminded of the psalmist who said, "Thy seat is like as the sun before me" (Ps. 89:35, BCP).

One personal detail of my pilgrimage I will disclose to you. I found, and still find, that much initiative in saying prayers has been taken from me. Instead I have been gratefully conscious of a surging tide of prayers for me and my recovery, and I have relaxed and "floated" along with that tide, passively. The Psalter, which, as many of you have realized, I know pretty well by heart, drifts into my consciousness and out again and always refreshes and invigorates my soul. The blessed sacrament received every day at the hands of one of my colleagues and the quiet thanksgiving I can make for that unspeakable gift have been the source of tremendous joy.

There is no room for rage or a desire for vengeance on my part or anybody else's, still less for depression or melancholy. Others have experienced worse, have had more broken bones and much more pain, more scars, and infinitely more disablement. I have merely joined the crowd of witnesses to pain and crime in this city after sixteen years totally free of any fright or injury of any personal sort.

And be assured that there are no nightmares, no bad dreams, no fearful memories. I saw nothing of the man who attacked me. I never heard him. I remember nothing unpleasant. I have from the bottom of my heart forgiven him, so what is there to be bitter about or to resent? For the Lord's love has not diminished, and his power to heal has been proved to me, miraculously, strongly. The psalmist knew it when he wrote, "If I climb up into heaven, Thou art there; if I make my bed in hell, Thou art there also" (Ps. 139:7). I know this to be true, as I know this next piece of Scripture to be true also, triumphantly and eternally so: "If God be for us, who can be against us?" (Rom. 8:31, KJV).

Between a Rock and a Hard Place

You would not be surprised if I were to tell you that I have given a good deal of thought this week to what happened a year ago on Friday the eighteenth, when I was coming home from a dinner given for a black priest friend of mine — a good deal of thought and many prayers of gratitude to a gracious and loving God whose healing was deemed miraculous by the two surgeons who saw to certain matters for me. But the pulpit is to be used for talking about God and not about being half-murdered.

I want to take you into my confidence and point to what I think I see about the divine activity in situations where at first sight you would not expect God's love to be much in evidence. We have been reminded — jolted is a better term — by the lessons read in the liturgy today. I watched you listening to them and sensing a certain cold comfort in them both. They talk of standards — frighteningly inflexible standards — of the divine righteousness which are the core of truth. Do you remember:

> Let the prophet who has a dream tell the dream, but let him who has my word speak my word faithfully. What has straw in common with wheat? says the LORD. Is not my word like fire . . . and like a hammer which breaks the rock in pieces?

> Jeremiah 23:28-29

There isn't much room in that passage for any Crystal Cathedral type of reassurance about self-esteem. The statement is appalling. He puts us in our place — firmly, by putting himself in his. What has our straw in common with his wheat, indeed? What we dream up to say doesn't of itself have the life-filled, life-filling seed: our attempts are dry and hollow and, when you come to think of it, finally worthless. What can you do with straw? Stuff mattresses or thatch roofs or add some wet clay to make bricks, but that's about it. But wheat is a living organism that in its turn gives life in nourishment. Only God's word gives whole life.

Then the imagery about God's ineffable holiness becomes more intense. "Is not *my* word like fire . . . and like a hammer which breaks the rock in pieces?" Fire separates gold from dross. The baser materials burn up and the gold remains. Fire gets to the bottom of things. It destroys, reduces. At the bottom is the gold, "purified seven times in the fire," as the psalmist says. It is God's word that reveals the indestructible, displays the final substance, provides the inescapable evidence, assures the unavoidable discovery. That indestructible, that final substance, that inescapable evidence, that unavoidable discovery, that purest of refined gold is the truth. The divine fire is the divine judgment.

The divine hammer will break the rock to reveal the vein of gold. It will display the truth, bring it to the light of day. Divine judgment.

And in the Gospel reading you heard a few minutes ago, Christ says, "I have come to cast fire upon the earth" (Luke 12:49, RSV): he is speaking of the divine judgment.

And then, the cost of truth. The cost of truth is division.

Do you suppose I came to establish peace upon the earth? No, indeed, I have come to bring division. For from now on, five members of a family will be divided, three against two and two against three; father against son and son against father, mother against daughter and daughter against mother,

mother against son's wife, and son's wife against her mother-in-law.

Luke 12:51-53, NEB

We can understand the mother-in-law bit, but what about the rest? The rest sits uncomfortably with us. Family unity is important. It is an American virtue. In England, family loyalties can become a snobbish talisman. You can imagine what effect these words had on the Jewish families of Christ's day.

Now do you understand the meaning of a saying we often use: between a rock and a hard place? We find ourselves between a rock and a hard place when we take Christ seriously. Fire and metal. Go back to Jeremiah. Listen again to what God is saying through him: "Is not my word like fire . . . and like a hammer which breaks the rock in pieces?" Are we not told that God's word is none other than Christ himself, the Word of God?

So Christ is warning that part of the evidence of his activity among those who take him seriously and let him live in their lives is the possibility — no, the probability — of deep division. The individual decision to allow him into your life is inescapable. Therein lies the division. We shall be put between a rock and a hard place.

And as between one person and another, so within our individual lives. This is the bad news for all the institutions we erect and all the assumptions we adopt. Nothing is safe anymore from the inexorable demands of truth and righteousness, from expectations of integrity in what we plan and accomplish, because there is no winking, no blinking of the attention from the God who "neither slumbers nor sleeps." You can't paper over the cracks with Christ. You can't brush it under the carpet with Christ. You can't shove it into the catch-all closet until he's gone, hide it under the sofa cushion and sit on it. You can't "keep it in the family,"

173

for the family, Christ tells us, is the very place, the very unit, where his demands for truth will make themselves most deeply felt. Allegiance to him, recognition of his place in the life of a believer, can undermine even that, and will. We know from history it will.

I have tried to be faithful to the Scriptures set for you to listen to and for me to preach upon today. They are bleak. They may disturb you. They scare the living daylights out of me, because I know that in what I am, every bit as much as in what I do, I am between a rock and a hard place. Christ is hammering away at the rocky accretions that I have been successful in making around the things I cherish most about myself in my life, from preferences to friendships, from unkind judgments to self-aggrandizing ambition, from envies I sustain to cowardly fears I entertain, from acquisitiveness with people as well as possessions — from all the hard-shell attempts to receive him on my terms and not his. God sends his word, Christ himself, the hammer, the fire in my straw.

But there is another way. Christ wants us to see this. He is *not* absent from situations in which at first you might not expect his love to be much in evidence. Go back to the Scriptures, back to Jeremiah: "Am I a God at hand, says the LORD, and not a God afar off? Can a man hide himself in secret places so that I cannot see him? . . . Do I not fill heaven and earth?" (Jer. 23:23, RSV). In other words, the divine activity, the saving work of Christ, is not deterred or deflected by the hardness of heart, the contempt for his word and commandments, the passion for isolation from his loving care on our part. He is present in the heart of the division *he* creates. He divides only in order to heal. He destroys only in order to build. He burns only in order to raise up newer and stronger life. This is hard for us to take in, for we are either motivated by or respond to resentment, anger, jealousy, revenge, and lustful desire, and our best selves are not present, not much in evidence, in divisions *we* create when we cause hurt or grief or any occasion of separation and distress or when literally we injure or maim another of God's children.

Which brings me around to the reference I made at the beginning of this sermon. As I pause to thank God for his infinite mercies toward me at this time, for healing and restoration and strength, I realize with a legion of his children that Christ has been *there*, within the wounds I sustained and in the weakness that became my daily diet for some weeks, in the physical separation from my beloved parish family and in the forgiveness I was required from the ground of my heart freely to offer my attacker. At the heart of that particular storm Christ's companionship made itself keenly evident to me, none other than that same companionship that hammers the rock of my heart to divide me from my lesser self, to bring to the light of his new morning his truth embedded within me as within every other soul who owns him as Savior and the Word of God.

Obedience Training

Humanity has long known just how delicious forbidden fruit can taste. See a notice marked PRIVATE on a doorway, and you have opened it and possibly gone in. See a letter stamped STRICTLY CONFIDENTIAL, and you have broken its seal and its secrecy and shared its contents with colleagues or friends or lovers. It only takes a request that you not walk on the grass to get you to walk on it. Mankind, the Scriptures tell us, "is born to trouble as the sparks fly upward" (Job 5:7, RSV). And I am being literal-minded when I add that this is *sure as hell* true. We have the itch to disobey. An itch isn't a rational activity: we react to it. All that is necessary to get your libido to heat up if not boil over is to be told that you are not to commit adultery. Things forbidden fascinate. Our predisposition is to disobey. We set our judgments and what we fondly call "our needs" over and above commandments, requirements, orders, and the advice of those who are older and wiser, and, without regard to our peril, we go on our way rejoicing, to have *our way*.

You heard what the children of Israel got up to when Moses' back was turned. They couldn't wait.

They have turned aside quickly out of the way which I commanded them; they have made for themselves a molten calf, and have worshiped it and sacrificed to it, and said,

"These are your gods, O Israel, who brought you up out of the land of Egypt!"

Exodus 32:8, RSV

It is hard to believe that they could have been such fools, such ungrateful fools, in the face of their miraculous deliverance, but take a look at their track record up to then for doubting their integrity as the covenanted people of God. It is a lamentable catalogue of disobedience and grudging acquiescence. They were a pack of recidivists, sliding back to their illegalities. William Temple was right on target, I think, when he said that every revelation of God is a demand, and the way to knowledge of God is by obedience. It seems as if they were set against ever learning anything about their loving God whose revelation of his caring and mighty arm outstretched to save had been so dramatically evident to them and to their oppressors.

"Every revelation of God is a demand, and the way to knowledge of God is by obedience." Get around that if you can. The point is, you can't. Remember Christ's own baptism by John in the Jordan and the divine revelation in those dread words: "This is my beloved Son in whom I am well pleased." The demand is intrinsic in the revelation: believe him. He will say what he will say because he is what he is: my beloved Son.

What does he say? He says a lot about obedience — not least, his own. John records it for us: "I can do nothing on my own authority. . . . I seek not my own will but the will of him who sent me" (John 5:30, RSV). He says a lot about obedience. John tells us that later he said, "he who has my commandments and keeps them, he it is who loves me; and he who loves me will be loved by my Father, and I will love him and manifest myself to him" (John 14:21, RSV).

And do we not know how he lived his own obedience out, how he "became obedient unto death, even the death

177

of the cross"? (Phil. 2:8, KJV). That life, that suffering, that death, yes, and his resurrection, constituted the obedience the divine covenant required. His is what Paul describes as the "obedience of the one" (Rom. 5:19) which ensures our destiny, if we believe on him.

His obedience, the author of the letter to the Hebrews tells us, enabled him to fulfill the role of High Priest perfectly: "Although he was a Son, he learned obedience through what he suffered; and being made perfect he became the source of eternal salvation *to all who obey him,* being designated by God a high priest after the order of Melchizedek" (Heb. 5:9-10, RSV).

"All who obey him"? All who take his claims seriously in their lives, who want him to live in them, who *ask* him to live in them: "O come to my heart, Lord Jesus; there is room in my heart for thee."

Now, I have stated the theological premise. I have sketched the theological pattern on the canvas for you. And you can see what a large canvas it is. Nor is it necessarily one we want to have around to look at. Because we don't welcome obedience as a concept. We like to walk through doorways marked PRIVATE. We like to read letters stamped CONFIDENTIAL. We like to walk on the grass. And — apply this generally — forbidden sexual fruit seems fascinating and tasty to us: like the Hebrews of old, we sit down to eat and drink of it, to rise up to play our own game. Self-will is the name of that game.

The priests at St. Thomas have a clergy colleague whom we tease for referring to life's *unmanageability* in most sermons. Having heard the term so often, I've frequently pondered what it can comprise. Life's unmanageability doesn't always mean one's inability to cope with a hostile environment; it can mean the mess we make at trying to deal with it because we insist on using the wrong tools, applying the wrong rules, taking liberties with the laws that so delicately govern its balance, and putting self first every time — in fact, doing everything we can possibly imagine to avoid the concept of obedience.

Being Anglican, Episcopalian, Christians doesn't necessarily make the problem easier either. The reluctance to wield an authoritarian stick, whether through insisting on a fundamentalist interpretation of Holy Scripture or through hierarchical sanctions, is part of our heritage. We are not in the habit of Bible thumping or of compelling intellectual and moral compliance because we know that

> a soul convinced against its will
> will hold the same opinion still,

and unwilling obedience, grudging acquiescence, foot-dragging compliance, is of little real value. We are not punished if we doubt. We aren't expelled if we withhold assent to prime doctrines of the Christian faith. We can even preach our refusal and get away with it.

All the more reason, because of the large room in which the Lord has set our Anglican feet, for looking hard at how we use our latitude, our freedoms to obey. Examine our lifestyles. Are they in conformity with Christ's reminders to strive for holiness and truth? Examine Christ's hopes and expectations for unity of his church in holiness and truth, and ask yourself whether you are impeding that unity for which he prayed. *Is* obedience an issue that we have examined and applied? Are you hoping and intending to "grow into the measure of the stature of the fullness of Christ" by God's grace? If not, why are you here? Only obedience can make you receptive to the grace you will need.

Is penitence a part of your life? It is a sign of obedience to a loving lawgiver and ruler in God. Is generosity a part of your life? It is a sign of obedience to a generous God and life-giver. Is compassion a part of your life? It is a sign of obedience to the One who was God who came to where we are, who deprived himself to take on humanity and manhood for our sake, and who has taken it back with him as the consummate act of compassion for our fallen and redeemed state. Is humility part of your life? It is a sign of obedience to the Son who humbled himself and took the form of a servant.

Here then is the challenge and the hope. You are entitled to both if you take Christ seriously. For you can know him, and knowing him, you will know the truth: the thing that will set you free.

One Last Chance

There was a rude expression my family employed when someone was slow to grasp a point in conversation: "Use a hammer."

Christ Jesus had not been brought up by the carpenter Joseph for nothing. He knew that you had to hit a nail on the head several times before it went to where it was supposed to be. Listen again to what he's trying to drive home in the Gospel reading we heard as the second lesson: "Unless you repent, you will, all of you come to the same end" (Luke 13:3, NEB). "Unless you repent, you will all of you, come to the same end" (Luke 13:5, NEB). "If it bears next season, well and good; if not, you shall have it down" (Luke 13:9, NEB).

Three times in nine verses: not a threat but a promise. Either the fruits of repentance — or destruction. Repentance from what? Turning away from what? The people to whom he was talking both directly and in the parable were his fellow countrymen. They were endangering themselves. They were risking their existence by impenitence. They were simply not coming to terms with God's requirements that they show awareness of wrongdoing and plan to do something about it by turning back to him, by producing fruits of repentance.

Christ is hammering home the generous offer of God to give them one last chance. One Last Chance. This is entirely in the character and personality of God to "save to the uttermost," as Scripture says.

One last chance. God has been offering this to succeeding generations through the recorded history of his loving dealings with us. The prophet Jeremiah shouted the same offer: "O Jerusalem, wash your heart from wickedness, that you may be saved" (Jer. 4:14, RSV).

A couple of weeks ago I preached about the rainbow that God sent as a sign of his covenant with the people to whom he had given one last chance with the flood — with Noah and his family on the ark. They had listened and had taken advantage of God's offer. The rainbow he sent was the seal on the agreement God had come to with Noah.

The point is that God's love is such that it is ceaselessly active to elicit a response from us. He never tires from his desire to call from us the love that his love has planted in our hearts. His respect for us is to be seen in the freedom of response he has bestowed upon us. Our attitude to him — the attitude of all creation — always derives from the posture of response. With him always lies the initiative. He is the well and fountain of that love which initiates and prompts creation — its sustenance, its growth, its encouragement, its flowering, its achievement of the potential he has planted.

But there is a snag: we are free to withhold the response his loving initiative is calling from us. Just listen to this, from St. Luke's Gospel, if you want to see what I mean.

> When they heard him, all the people, including the tax-gatherers, praised God, for they had accepted John's baptism; but the Pharisees and lawyers, who refused his baptism, had rejected God's purpose for themselves.

Christ goes on:

> 'How can I describe the people of this generation? What are they like? They are like children sitting in the market-place

and shouting at each other, "We piped for you and you would not dance." "We wept and wailed, and you would not mourn.'"

Luke 7:29-32, NEB

There it is. The refusal to respond to God's loving initiative and purpose for us. The comparison Christ makes to the children in the marketplace can clearly be a description of the contemporary state of human affairs. What he says is still where it's at, if I may use that inelegant expression.

There we have the tug and pull of the tireless, unwearying, eternal will and wish of a loving Creator to elicit a loving, free response from his creatures — and the creatures using that same freedom to withhold that loving response.

God pipes for us, and we will not dance. The music goes on, but no one wants to dance to God's tune. We talk lightly of freedom. We ought "seriously to lay to heart the dangers we are in by our unhappy divisions," as Archbishop William Laud put it in his prayer for Christian unity, the dangers we are in because of our selfish understanding of freedom. We must recall that we have the freedom *not* to respond to God's loving purposes only because he offered it to us as a gift.

Look more closely at how dangerous, how destructive that freedom not to respond can be. With this freedom, as with all else, if we've got it, we flaunt it. And when God's love is conveyed to us through others — our parents and siblings, perhaps; our children and partners, certainly; our lovers and friends, certainly — when God's love is conveyed in this way, to and through these people, and we withhold our free response of love to them, we wreck the fragile and sensitive mechanism by which our place in this world is sweetened, and by which theirs is sweetened also.

183

Scarcely anything is more defeating, frustrating, and finally embittering than being denied love, having love withheld. Where there should be music, there is silence. Where there should be sunlight, there is shadow. Where there should be warm fire, there are cold ashes. It is an area where nothing healthy can grow, no life can be sustained. The wonder of it all is that God should have taken the risk that his love would not be returned, reflected in the lives of his creatures, when he gave us the freedom to withhold it if we will.

We have experienced love grown cold. Our lives are pockmarked with the traces of it. We have ceased to love someone or allowed a love to die, perhaps having ourselves blown out the flame of love out of a fear of the commitment it entailed or because we were more attracted to someone else, to a love that excited us more, intrigued us more, gave us more of what we thought we were looking for. Or we may have experienced it happening to us. The devastation of no longer being loved, the misery of never having been really loved by parents or family or people we hoped so much would love us is life-wrecking. Before you do it to anybody else, remember our Lord's three-hit point you heard me read to you today. God has the right, with all the freedom he has given us, to expect a free response of grateful love to him. Why? Christ tells us why. God has made us capable of experiencing his joy: "My joy shall be in you, that your joy may be full" (John 15:11).

If we don't come to that experience because we withhold our love, we won't *live*. We may exist. We may take up space in a family, in a community, in a productive economy, but we won't be living. We may be successful, we may wield power, we may figure in a nation's history, but we won't live. We choose to exclude ourselves from life when we thwart God's purpose within us to reflect his love. When God pipes for us and we do not dance, let us not blame him if we become too stiff to move at all, too blind to see the dance floor, and too lonely to feel the hand of a partner who invites us to join in. For that is what will happen: this is what Christ is saying will happen. He is offering us one last chance. He is offering us one last dance.

The Dynamics of Conversion

On Friday morning of this past week a descendant of a long line of Presbyterian ministers came to see me about becoming an Anglican. His antecedents were a remarkable blend of Welsh and Italian — all the charm and creativity and musicality melded from those two nations: Celt and Mediterranean. It set me thinking.

If I were in the habit of asking you to raise your hands in answer to questions I put to you from the pulpit, you might not like it, but you might learn a lot from the crowds who come here. Don't worry. That isn't part of this morning's sermon exercise, nor has the vicar thought it a seemly addition to the liturgy. But he may. I wonder how many of you are converts from some other denomination, or some other faith, or from no faith or belief at all, to Anglicanism, the Episcopal denomination of the Christian faith? Quite a lot. How do I know? I'll tell you how I know. Every time we begin our inquirers' classes for confirmation, we have people approach us from all the Christian denominations you can think of: from the Protestants, like Lutherans, Methodists, Presbyterians, Baptists, and Congregationalists. From the Quakers. From Seventh Day Adventists. From the Catholic wing of the church: Romans, Greek Orthodox, Russian Orthodox, Serbian Orthodox. Polish National Catholics. From Judaism. From unbelief of one sort or another. The proportion of converts in the Anglicanism of this country is very interestingly high.

The *dynamic* of conversion is very interesting. I found myself thinking this on Friday morning when that young man told me he wanted to shift allegiances to the Catholic stream, to us. What is it, do you think, that draws people away from one set of beliefs, or no religion at all, to another set of beliefs? Gone are the days, thank God, when the Episcopal Church was thought to be the church for the socially respectable. Can you imagine that people would actually "upgrade," so to speak, their religious denomination when they were upwardly mobile, when they moved into a nicer neighborhood, when they started getting their suits tailored instead of buying them off the rack or started going to a more fashionable dress shop, when they were hoping to get into an exclusive club? Membership in the Episcopal Church was supposed to top it all off. Some topping! But I guess people did it, and I suppose some people still do. The good Lord understands it, and, along with all the rest of our human frailty and vanities and pretensions, he redeems it even if he doesn't overlook it. Nowadays the Episcopal Church embraces every color and ethnic background. Numerically, Anglicanism is a Third World church, with more black members around the world than white. And despite its origins, it is rightly and curiously *un*English. It is far from being socially desirable any longer, far from being as socially influential as once it was in this country or anywhere. It is far from being what I once saw a boarding house in Seabright, New Jersey, advertised as: "a nice house for nice people."

But the question of the *dynamic* of conversion, the whole business of embracing one faith or another faith or another form of the same faith, making the decision to take that leap, is what lies before us to consider. Why consider it? Look at the Scripture set for today's worship.

Naomi, the widow, discovers that she now has two widows for daughters-in-law. These two women had not merely married into the family; they had married into the family religion. Listen: the two sons "took them wives of the women of Moab" (Ruth 1:4, KJV) in which they had gone to live from Bethlehem in Judah, with their godly father, Elimelech. We know he was godly. His name tells us so: "God is king." That name is important. Ruth, his daughter-in-law, came from paganism into contact with godliness when she married one of his sons. To what extent this old man's influence affected her we can gather from that superb protest she makes to her mother-in-law Naomi as the old lady plans to return to Bethlehem, the home she had left in the famine — words I learned as a child of six in my village school in Yorkshire:

> Intreat me not to leave thee, or to return from following after thee: for whither thou goest I will go; and where thou lodgest I will lodge: thy people shall be my people, and thy God my God: Where thou diest, will I die, and there will I be buried: the LORD do so to me, and more also, if ought but death part thee and me.

Ruth 1:16-17, KJV

Ruth was a convert to her father-in-law's religion. Why? Because the old man had made his faith real to her. She realized and recognized his God. The recognition, the realization, was not merely important to her; it was relevant. It spoke to her soul. It rang true and it made her restless until she embraced it. People are converted when they are gripped by the love that will not let them go until they return it in the way it has been given. I am thinking about that young man who wants to embrace Anglicanism. Something in it rings true for him, truer than what he has known so far, and true enough to make him want to do something about it.

People are converted by a recognition of something not merely true but vital to their existence and the life of their soul. The soul requires fulfillment every bit as much as your bodily needs require fulfillment. There are times when we gorge the latter and starve the former, but the imbalance, the starvation, will not be endured if it is peace inside that you need. The soul-starvation can make itself powerfully felt, and it can propel the heart and the mind, on occasions against one's will, to make a decision of commitment, a turning to, a turning from, to the embracing of a new direction, as a magnetized needle, if balanced on a fulcrum, will swing to the magnetic North, at first slowly as though unwilling, and then with deliberate certainty.

I am now thinking about two other people, one you don't know, and someone you may know by name. The first is an Oxford classmate of mine, David Mawer. He came up to Keble College from his prep school with an earned reputation for swift intelligence, a sharp tongue, scant respect for the church, and less so for those like myself preparing to serve full time in it. He was and still is a fine pianist. I found him one day pounding the living daylights out of his piano in fury and frustration. "What do you think you're doing? You'll break the thing," I managed to yell. He yelled back: "I'm trying to drown God's voice. He won't stop telling me he wants me to be a priest." Thirty-five years later he celebrates the thirtieth anniversary of his ordination. He came to it kicking and struggling.

Listen now to C. S. Lewis:

> You must picture me alone in that room in Magdalene [College, Oxford] night after night, feeling, whenever my mind lifted even for a second from my work, the steady, unrelenting approach of Him whom I so earnestly desired not to meet. In the Trinity Term of 1929, I gave in and admitted that God was God, and knelt and prayed; perhaps, that night, the most dejected and reluctant convert in all England.

Surprised by Joy, p. 133

Or you can read the majestic poem "The Hound of

189

Heaven" about that relentless pursuit, and the capture. It
begins:

> I fled Him, down the nights and down the days;
> I fled Him, down the arches of the years . . .

and it ends

> Halts by me that footfall:
>   Is my gloom, after all,
> Shade of His hand, outstretched caressingly?
>   'Ah, fondest, blindest, weakest,
>   I am He whom thou seekest!
> Thou dravest love from thee, who dravest Me!'

Francis Thompson

Think again now about the ten men with leprosy healed
by Christ on obeying his command to go and show themselves to the priests, and one of them, not a Jew but a
Samaritan, "turned back," we are told, praising God aloud.
Here was literally a conversion — a turning to face the
healer who in healing had made God real to him, and in
turning back, in being converted, was not merely healed of
his disease but *made whole,* which is what conversion can
do, and in God's mercy, *will.*

This phenomenon is usually less of an event than an
activity, a progressive, sustained bringing into line of all that
you have and are. For the reality gradually, under the loving-
kindness of God, becomes more and more clear, as the
wayward and untoward tendencies, preferences, prejudices,
and self-willed nonsense that clutter the soul are disciplined,
brought to heel, told to keep quiet, get lost, drop dead by
that soul as its love for the reality increasingly absorbs its
attention.

And worship assists it, both private and public. You
couldn't imagine this process without resorting to talk to
the God to whom you turn, listening for his voice, trying to

understand what his will for you happens to be. He can speak to you, make himself real to you, in the quiet of your room as you read the Scriptures or think about him. This is exactly what happened to a young medical student who was reading St. Mark's Gospel through and was aware as he was finishing it that Christ was standing at the other side of his table. That man is the Russian Orthodox Archbishop Anthony Bloom. God can speak to you, make himself real to you, as you give yourself in the worship of some great liturgy. And there are people sitting in those pews beside you who can tell you how true that is. There are literally Christmas and Easter converts in this congregation to whom at that time Christ has made his reality known, for worship at its best not only leads us from the known to the unknown but brings people to the stage where they are reminded of God's majesty and, beyond that, to the point that they can actually see glimpses of it. Think about that, about the holy magic this past Holy Week of the Tenebrae which brought us close indeed to our suffering Lord in its severity and simplicity.

Our job is, as far as we can, to make the reality of God known through the worship of this place. It means that we can take nothing for granted; we cannot afford to sit on our laurels. The challenge of this conversion potential goads and haunts me and all of us, and we must not rest until we view it as our primary task here, until people catch that vision from us. That task will never end, for the story of this place is that people come, and some are convicted and converted by the experience.

So we try. Occasionally, I think, we may fail. But we have no mandate to cease trying. The conversion dynamic is very powerful and very delicate, and we don't want to get in its way. More music than ever is being sung by our remarkable choir, at evensongs on Thursdays as well as Tuesdays. It may help your conversion further. I pray that it will help my own, to strengthen my commitment to the Lord I love and serve so poorly. For we are meant to "grow into the measure of the stature of the fullness of Christ" in this part of the church where we find ourselves and, growing, to help make that reality plain for those who join us and who may recognize it also as their home. And stay, rejoicing!

The Short Fuse

I am speaking to those of you who like myself have what we call a "short fuse." So I am going to preach to myself all through this sermon.

Some folks are blessed with the great gift of quiet patience, and when they encounter situations they find unacceptable, uncongenial, or perhaps unnatural to their temperament, they don't acquiesce, they don't condone, they don't comply, but they accept these situations, perhaps suffering in silence, and eventually emerge none the weaker for their unwelcome experience. Others, like myself, are less gifted. They find restraint irksome, unpalatable situations unbearable, and typically these feelings manage to make themselves evident. It doesn't always improve the situation, much less solve the problem.

For instance, I don't know about you but I find the psalm set for today highly embarrassing — embarrassing because it speaks to my short fuse and accuses me:

> Fret not thyself because of the ungodly;
>> neither be thou envious against the evil doers.
> For they shall be cut down like the grass;
>> and be withered even as the green herb. . . .
> Grieve not thyself at him, whose way doth prosper,
>> against the man that doeth after evil counsels.

> Leave off from wrath, and let go displeasure:
> fret not thyself, else shalt thou be moved to do evil.

Psalm 37:1-2, 7-8, BCP

There it is. Holy wisdom suggests that the short fuse when it ignites burns the aggravator and the aggrieved both.

Let this be said: there is much to ignite that fuse. Righteous indignation does have its place. When politicians and people in positions of public privilege and responsibility cheat, take bribes, get their money mixed up with the firm's, talk hypocritically about drugs; when preachers who have pointed to the sexual sins and failures of their colleagues are discovered themselves to have indulged in extracurricular pursuits of the same sort; when greed for millions on Wall Street is exposed and the white-collar lawbreakers plead that they have done nothing more than made mistakes, righteous indignation does have its place. You have heard me say this before, but I think it can be said again: you make a mistake when there are two identical coats hanging next to each other and you grab the one that isn't yours. But you know perfectly well what your wife or husband looks like, and if you pick up another wife or husband to go home with, that isn't a mistake: that is a sin. Righteous indignation *does* have a place in the face of flagrant cheating, whether social or sexual or financial, or of flagrant injustice and marginalization and discrimination.

You remember our Lord's own reaction to the desecration of his Father's house in Jerusalem: he charged among the money changers, flailing a scourge and scattering tables and chairs as he chased them and those who were selling animals for sacrifice from the sacred precincts. There was little of the live-and-let-live, shrug-the-shoulder stuff there. And souls alight with his love can burn a similar indignation at the bestiality of conditions they see others reduced to — like William Blake, appalled by the "dark, Satanic mills" of

194

England in the early days of the Industrial Revolution and by the misery of those consigned to sweat in them:

> Bring me my bow of burning gold!
> Bring me my arrows of desire!
> Bring me my spear! O clouds, unfold!
> Bring me my chariot of fire!
> I will not cease from mental fight;
> Nor shall my sword slip in my hand,
> 'Til we have built Jerusalem
> In England's green and pleasant land.

And we have among us those who are incensed by the poverty and the misery that both begets and inherits the sale of death-dealing drugs in the streets of our cities. Yes, righteous indignation does have its place.

But I don't think that this is what the psalmist is referring to. If you look at the text carefully, you can see that it's not so much a case of righteous indignation as of not allowing God his rightful prerogative — in other words, playing God at his own game. Far better is it to "put thou thy trust in the LORD, and be doing good; dwell in the land, and verily thou shalt be fed. Delight thou in the LORD, and he shall give thee thy heart's desire. Commit thy way unto the LORD, and put thy trust in him, and he shall bring it to pass. He shall make thy righteousness as clear as the light. . . . Hold thee still in the LORD, and abide patiently upon him" (Ps. 37:3-7, BCP).

All the time you can hear the steady emphasis on the divine prerogative, on allowing God to do his good creative and redemptive work.

And then in verse 11 comes the cue, the key word that holds the point of the psalm together: "The meek-spirited shall possess the earth; and shall be refreshed in the multitude of peace." That is what is required of those of us with a short fuse.

And now let us turn to the Old Testament reading set for this morning's worship, where the prophet Micah recounts God's gentle remonstrance of the Lord with his people, recalling his redemptive work among them: "O my people, what have I done unto thee? And wherein have I wearied thee? . . . For I brought thee up out of the land of Egypt, and returned thee out of the house of servants" (Mic. 6:3-4, KJV). You heard these words end that reading: "He hath shewed thee, O man, what is good; and what doth the LORD require of thee, but to do justly, and to love mercy, and to walk humbly with thy God?" (Mic. 6:8, KJV). There it is again: allow God to do his good creative and redemptive work by cooperating with him, walking humbly with him. The meek shall possess the earth.

Which is what Christ is saying in the Beatitudes, using these precise words, taken from the psalms learned by heart as a boy: "Blessed are the meek: for they shall inherit the earth" (Matt. 5:5, KJV).

Let us come back to the righteous anger that I mentioned earlier. Is it not possible that the meek soul is the soul that is angry at the right time and never angry at the wrong time — angry when others are injured, when injustice seems to triumph, when cruelty reigns, but not angry at personal injury or humiliation? I can personally attest that anger at personal injury can and will retard healing, thanks be to God. William Barclay tells us that the word *meek* in Greek has an intriguing meaning: it is used of animals that have been trained to obey a command. So the meek can be properly understood not as those who are self-controlled but as those who are God-controlled. I like that. In his will is our peace. In his service is perfect freedom. A meek soul can claim that.

And the secret is humility, walking humbly with your God. Now that is an elusive grace. You can't acquire it. For goodness' sake don't search among those self-help books in the shops for the title *Humility: How to Achieve It in Six Weeks*. If you find the book, don't buy it. Do you know how it is learned? By being humiliated. So unless you're prepared for that, don't pray for the grace of humility to be given you. The great saints have paid a great price in being given it. It was said of the brave Edmund Campion, the Jesuit martyr under Queen Elizabeth I, that he "was a man of many parts, though he who rode post to tell him so would arrive too late to bring him tidings thereof." He was arrogant. But he was humiliated, and he learned meekness, the meekness of Christ, as he underwent untold sufferings in his torture and his death for love of Christ.

The trouble with the English language is that time can fade its color. To us in a thrusting, achieving, acquisitive, and competitive New York, meekness does not seem to be much of a virtue. We associate it with behavior that is cowardly and craven. But this is wrong. Meekness is in fact the sign of great inner strength, for which we might use another misunderstood word, *gentleness*. It is associated with strong convictions, strong opinions even, strong priorities, strong loyalties, expressed in such a way that God's love can shine through them, as it shone through a brave and chivalrous character whom Geoffrey Chaucer in his *Canterbury Tales* described as "A very parfit gentil knight."

God and the Knife

Get ready when Christ uses word pictures. You heard him saying this morning that his Father is the gardener. He is not telling us that God is a nice old guy in a straw hat with a hoe in his hand. He is telling us that God has very sharp eyes and a knife in his hand. God prunes; he cuts away. Listen again: "Every barren branch of mine he cuts away; and every fruiting branch he cleans, to make it more fruitful still" (John 15:2, NEB).

We tend to turn our heads away from discussions of God's strictness, of his using drastic measures. But Christ wants us to face facts. The facts are these. If you claim the privilege of the title "Christian," you stand right in the path of those sharp eyes and that keen knife. For Christ is the real vine, he says, and we are the branches. But branches have an obligation if they are going to remain branches and not become kindling: you have to be productive. If you don't produce, the knife will separate you from your claimed relationship to that vine. This is not what *might* happen: this is what *will* happen. Christ says so. And even when we think we're being useful, even when we assume we're being productive, along comes that knife to cut us down to size, for we are not as mature as we think, and the gardener's task is to prune back the potentially productive immature branches in order to increase productivity. The branch is not allowed to try to produce fruit for the first few years. It is cut back, cut back, cut back before it is given the opportunity to produce.

Pain and separation are intrinsic to the Christian life. It is always to some extent *uncertain.* You can't claim "blessed assurance: Jesus is mine" without conceding that Jesus is no cozy teammate, no cherished possession. There is an element of discomfort always, an element of uncertainty at what God expects from us. In that relationship there is the possibility of disappointment.

Our previous mayor, Mr. Ed Koch, had a habit of asking people, "How'm I doin'?" It was supposed to be an endearing part of his self-confident nature that he would allow himself to appear to listen to people rate his progress. He probably thought he was doin' just fine. He may also have thought that the people of New York weren't in full knowledge of all the facts that governed his performance. Maybe he couldn't have cared less what people thought of how he was doin'. But he asked nonetheless. It was part of his winsomeness, a sort of chutzpah charm. And of course it brought the subject around to himself.

I'm not sure, having listened with some degree of apprehension and worry as St. John's account was read to us, that we are in any position to ask this of anyone about our Christian selves, our life in Christ. I *am* sure that we aren't in any position to address this blithe question to Christ. The question implies presumption of approval or at least a hope for approval. It asks for a smile of encouragement at least. But God didn't vote us in: he made us. "Thy hands have made me and fashioned me," said the psalmist. And as our Maker and Fashioner he knows whereof we are made and he is all too aware of how we're doin'. By and large we're not doin' too well. Frankly, we're not doin' well at all if we think for a moment we can do without the strong life that flows from the vine, his life in us, the source of all our life. We tend to forget that we are his creatures and that he has given us commandments. We must look at our creatureliness soberly and honestly, giving up any hope we have have of charming God into approving of what we have done with the good things he has given, and paying attention instead to what Paul tells the members of the church at Ephesus about God's terrifying generosity toward us. Nothing less than that. For left to ourselves, *left to ourselves,* we are in St. Paul's words, "dead in our sins" (Eph. 2:5, NEB). Try and duck that one.

Upon us, as upon his Son, God's mighty work of resurrection happens, if we claim Christ. "In Christ he has raised us up." We share Christ's resurrection life. That is terrifying generosity on the part of our Creator. Terrifying, because it places a yoke of responsibility upon us that we can't carry without Christ, who has said, "Come unto me, all ye that labor and are heavy laden, and learn of me, for my burden is easy and my yoke is light." That responsibility is *obedience*. We watch to see how Christ shoulders the yoke of obedience. With him at our side, we adjust our own. He helps us as we shoulder it. But it still hurts. He knows it hurts. It looks strangely like a cross. And then we remember that he expects us to shoulder our cross and follow him, with his.

Our obedience has a quality in it that Christ's does not need: penitence. For the question "How'm I doin'?" is the contrite-hearted question we are to ask not of God but of ourselves — secretly, soberly, sadly perhaps, as we look at him on the cross he has carried in front of us up the Calvary hill, and as we are carrying ours. Secretly, soberly, sadly perhaps, but hopefully and with trust, because he has conquered that death upon the cross and "ever liveth to make intercession for us." He is praying us through it, through the pruning, through the cutting back, through the cutting down to size, until in St. Paul's words we "come

into the measure of the stature of the fulness of Christ"
(Eph. 4:13).

I can do no other than place all this before you. Today's
Scripture selections made by the church leave me no choice.
There is no way that I can hope to take the sting out of
what Christ says. He portrays God as the gardener, with
keen eyes and a sharp knife. He claims to be the real vine
in himself, from which all life stems, and all hope. He leaves
no room for a sentimental anesthetic. It is for our good. Our
destiny is in him.

This brings me to the task of the church. What are we
here for? Why do we gather, Sunday by Sunday and week-
days as well? Worship however lovely with no impetus to
amend our lives or allow ourselves to submit to his pruning
is musically and liturgically self-indulgent. We should seek
to be challenged as we worship here at St. Thomas, to be
questioned as we participate, to be sobered as we listen and
convicted as we rejoice. It is one of the vineyards of the Lord
in this city, and the word is out: the Lord is not satisfied
with second best. He wants it all. He wants commitment to
him. He wants the best fruit we can produce. He wants our
highest productivity, to the glory of God. He wants his joy
to be in us that our joy may be full. He wants our generosity,
our glad companionship, not a few odd moments here or
an hour there. He wants our Magnificat, our song: "My
soul doth magnify the Lord, and my spirit hath rejoiced in
God my Savior." But not for our rejoicing alone.

He wants all this to have its harvest in the giving of
ourselves to those who need us, to those beyond our doors
whose lives are poorer and emptier of hope than ours. I
guess the term we should use is *compassion*: he wants us to
be increasingly aware of those marginalized by poverty or
ethnic difference or by lifestyles we find difficult to imagine
or understand or like, or by inadequacy of mind or intellect.
You know who I mean: the embarrassingly large numbers

of people who now live on our streets and sleep in our doorways and crowd the places that dispense free food and sustenance just in order to stay alive. Our pruning will increase an awareness, a compassion, an imagination for those who have less, have little, have nothing in common with the lives we live and the amenities we enjoy.

For to us is the promise that "If you dwell in me, and my words dwell in you, ask what you will, and you shall have it. This is my Father's glory, that you may bear fruit in plenty and so be my disciples" (John 15:7-8, NEB).

Frustration at the Gulf

If there is one thing that strikes with the force of a blow in that fascinating and beautiful and doomed country I have been in this past week, Israel, it is the phenomenon of fragmentation and separation. I had to go with two of my colleagues in the Order of St. John of Jerusalem (of which I'm the senior working member or provost in this country) in order to see the Ophthalmic Hospital, which our Order supports financially. It gave me an opportunity to compare and contrast impressions of the Holy City with those I received on a visit some twenty-five years ago. The separation and fragmentation I witnessed at the very heart of everything this time haunts me and supplies the background and the bones of the sermon based on the Scripture set for today.

You heard Isaiah proclaim what the Lord says to his people about those who love him despite their separation. Isaiah describes them as the "foreigners who join themselves to the LORD" (Isa. 56:6, RSV) and welcomes them. He wants them to share his love. God is not satisfied with separation and division. He does not accept man-made fragmentation. His love for his creation is inclusive, not exclusive. The lesson talks of those "foreigners" who love him, who "do justice and keep righteousness," who want to serve him and desire a life-link with him — a *covenant;* these he will bring to his holy mountain. Their sacrifices will be acceptable, and his house will bring joy to their prayers. "Thus says the LORD God, who gathers the outcasts of Israel, I will gather yet others . . . besides those already gathered" (Isa. 56:8, RSV). God proclaims his refusal to be narrow and selective in his welcome to those who seek him and yet are not within the confines of the Jewish covenant proper. It is a remarkable prophecy, a disturbing prophecy to those who bank on the fact of God being the God of the status quo. His love will not be "cribb'd, cabin'd and confin'd" to those who think it should be.

This is hard saying for many. People enjoy exclusivity when they're on the inside. But God, at the very heart of the inside of all things living, the Creator and Redeemer, wishes to bring all things to himself. He will not be deterred in his all-embracing love and welcome for those who respond with justice and righteousness and a desire to worship.

> Let not the foreigner who has joined himself to the LORD say, "The LORD will surely separate me from his people"; and let not the eunuch say, "Behold, I am a dry tree." For thus says the LORD: "To the eunuchs who keep my sabbaths, who choose the things that please me and hold fast my covenant, I will give in my house and within my walls a monument and a name better than sons and daughters; I will give them an everlasting name which shall not be cut off."

Isaiah 56:3-5, RSV

In language of high poetry, God proclaims his welcome for that most marginalized of human beings, a eunuch, to whom is denied the divine blessing of daughters and sons as his memorial. God will not endure separation and fragmentation of his creatures, his living souls.

Now turn to Paul. Remember Paul writes as a rabbi. He is used to turning a complicated phrase. Let us get one fact straight. What he is writing is a letter, not an essay. He dictates it to a secretary who races to put down what he hears. He hears a lot. Very probably he is walking up and down as he dictates. So you can hear anger at times, resentment at times, anxiety at times, assurance at times, persuasion at times, praise at times as he addresses *a particular situation* that requires his attention and action. It isn't a sort of vacation postcard we write: "Wish you were here; food not too bad; rains too much." He has something on his mind to tell. Whether the readers want to hear what he has to tell or not is of no consequence. He plunges in and argues his point.

He has a series of things on his agenda in this letter, one of which we briefly touch on in the Scripture set for this Sunday. He is writing, as he says, to non-Jewish people, the goyim, already detested by the ancient people of the covenant and now loathed because of their adherence to Christ. He calls them "a wild-olive shoot," grafted into the ancient tree that has had unfruitful branches broken off. He cautions them to be humble about their grafting and reminds those Gentile Christians that the broken Jewish branches can be and *should be,* grafted in again. "Note then the kindness and the severity of God. . . . For if you have been cut from what is by nature a wild olive tree, and grafted, contrary to nature, into a cultivated olive tree, how much more will these natural branches be grafted back into their own olive tree" (Rom. 11:22, 24, RSV).

He is saying that the separation and fragmentation between the people of Israel and the new Christians is something that can and should one day be resolved. God does not smile upon this cleavage between one set of people who love him and another. The gulf does not please him; it runs counter to his will and wish for his children, who should be part of the same living tree. The gulf is *not* fixed in God's eyes.

Now turn to St. Matthew's Gospel account of Christ and the Canaanite woman whose persistence and love surmounted the disciples' embarrassment at her shrieks for attention, the lack of response from Christ himself, and then his discouraging thrust about the little pet *dogs* — the word itself an insult used by Jews toward those like the Canaanites who were beyond the pale, marginalized, beyond the scope of Jewish concern or compassion. Her persistence was effective because she was quick on her feet, as you might say, and gave Jesus as good as she got: she made him laugh. He praised the faith and love that lay behind that persistence; he relished the light touch of her personality and the humor that was a by-product of her lively faith. And so he healed her daughter — a pagan, an "outcast of Israel," a foreigner marginalized and rejected by the Jewish people. It is an attractive story of the divine love undeterred by fragmentation embracing the undesirable, unwanted, and wrong-minded but seeking soul. She began her dealings with him under a political title: Son of David. She ended by kneeling at his feet and calling him Lord. She wanted for the very highest of all motives his love and healing in the direction of herself and her daughter. A daughter, not a cherished son, note, who might carry on the name. Pagan persistence led to a faithful recognition of who he was, and Christ grafted this wild olive shoot into the tree of the divine love and purpose.

All three Scripture readings carry the theme of marginalization, separation, fragmentation, and God's will and wish for them to fall into the divine embrace. Let us look at what I found last week in Israel. I had the chance to see and to hear and to discuss, at length, privately and publicly, what I saw and heard. What I saw and heard was and is a situation that, without divine help, will bring nothing other than death and destruction to the Holy Land. The facts are that in 1948 it was decided by the West that territory held and inhabited for two thousand years by Arabs, both Muslim and Christian, should be carved up and ceded to the Israeli people to set up a sovereign state. For centuries in their history the Jews had no country they could call their own. The Diaspora, a scattering of Jewish communities across the face of the earth, bears articulate testimony to this. They were given territory by a unilateral decision of powerful nations who were victors after the strife with Nazidom. But they found they had to fight for it. They had to fight the angry Arabs, resentful at being required to cede their territory, the lands they had thought their own, fields they had tilled and cultivated, houses they had built, communities they had constructed over centuries or millennia, buildings they had venerated, customs they had inherited, ways of thought they had been taught.

The intentions, ever since the Balfour Declaration in the early years of this century, were noble in concept: give the Jewish people opportunity to become a sovereign nation, an *entity,* a chance to realize their destiny — a divine destiny, they believe. And who that reads the Old Testament prophecies can question that? It was noble, but who besides the Jewish people were to pay the cost? The Arabs in the Holy Land had to pay the cost also. So an open wound of separation now festers, developing into fragmentation, as the refugee camps on the Gaza Strip bear witness. Behind road blocks, often surrounded by barbed wire and high metal fences erected to intercept stones thrown by frustrated and infuriated Arabs at the Israeli settlers, hundreds of thousands live in conditions that would horrify you. I have been there and seen the doctors working with these people on eye diseases and the increasing number of appalling eye injuries acquired in the uprising, or *intifada* as the uprising and violence is termed. I have been in their shanty homes with their leaky roofs, kitchens just a hole in a corner, sanitary provisions almost nonexistent, water supplies uncertain — in fact, all utilities likely to be severely cut if not cut off entirely as punishment for violence. Passes are required to leave the camps regularly for the scarce employment outside. Nineteen were living in one small house I saw; there were eleven in the barber's house next door. I saw a child with an artificial eye replacing one that was lost when it was hit by a rubber bullet in retaliation. True it is that small children soon become expert in stone throwing. True it is that people in the camps spend their time and sometimes their lives making explosive devices that sometimes blow up in their faces. True it is that most of them view Saddam Hussein as an Arab Robin Hood, a folk hero robbing the rich, arrogant, and uncaring Kuwaitis of their ill-gotten and greedily hoarded petroleum dollars and challenging the Arab world and the wicked West. True it is that hatred is as hot as a furnace in these fearful refugee camps. True it is that they believe violence to be the only way out of a situation they find suffocating and strangling.

And true it is that the hatred is matched and returned *in spades* by the Israeli powers, who will not tolerate protest of a policy of separation and marginalization (though some would deny that that is what their policy amounts to). There is a mean and vindictive separation of Israeli Jews and Arabs, and there is no immediate remedy in sight to cool the resentment or the furious determination on either side. I prophesy doom for that land unless and until by some godly miracle understanding is achieved of the concept of *redemption*.

And redemption is a Christian concept. Christ speaking of his own redemptive self-sacrifice on the cross says, "I, if I be lifted up, will draw all men to myself." Nothing else, no one else, can do this. Political arrangements can be arrived at, but true peace is founded only upon justice. Isaiah says, "Do justice." And is not *that* the piece of treasure lost in the dust of this house in which many people fight to claim as their own?

You've Got It All!

For one reason or another I seem to have more opportunity to watch the idiot's lantern — the television — than I remember having before. So I am becoming familiar with the latest advertisements on Channel 4. A funny little man sings a jingle that ends with the words, "You've got it all."

This could be said of the man who runs to Jesus in the story read for us this morning (Mark 10:17-27). He's got it all. All this, and heaven too. He knows he's got it all. He has great possessions. The Hebrews understood great wealth to be a sign that you are blessed by God. That is his first reassurance. His second is that his life is safe and sanitized. He hasn't murdered. He hasn't slept between the wrong sheets. He hasn't stolen. He hasn't borne false witness in a dispute. He hasn't done anybody out of anything that is rightfully theirs. He hasn't done dishonor to his father and mother. Sol Hurok, who was famous for getting things a little wrong, might have said that he is as clean as *a hen's tooth*. He's got it all. "All these things have I observed from my youth" (Mark 10:20, KJV).

So why, we may ask, does he throw himself at Christ's feet and ask "What must I do to inherit eternal life?" when he knows that he's got it all? Why? He has all the self-assurance of the well-endowed aristocracy, blessed by God and protected by adherence to the Ten Commandments of

209

Moses. Perhaps his youth — he still has his father and mother around — and his courtly good manners take him "over the top," as we would say, in enthusiasm for this fascinating charismatic teacher whose authority blazes more brightly than any scribe's. Perhaps he is just being polite. He knows he has all the necessary qualifications. But when Christ points out the small print to him, he cannot make a commitment.

One of the best pieces of worldly advice we can give or can get is to "read the small print." It saves much time and trouble and possibly much expense later. Father Ousley reminded me of an occasion when a second look I gave at the proof of my letter in the parish bulletin saved me untold embarrassment. There was a typographical error in the salutation; instead of "My dear Parishioners," the printer had put, "My dead Parishioners." *That,* with my signature at the end, would have taken a lot of unsaying, explaining, and pastoral contortion. Once you have committed yourself, whether in writing or in marriage or in any kind of activity in which others are involved, you are declared. Sitting on the fence should be left to that rare species of bird known as a mugwump; I am told that it sits with its mug on one side and its wump on the other.

But I am talking to a church full of people who have read the small print in your lives. Many of you are committed in the bond of marriage to somebody you love. It may be that your sense of commitment still stands with somebody whom for some reason you no longer love as you once did or who perhaps no longer loves you, but, having declared yourself, you stand by the commitment you once made. You may, some of you, have a commitment to some particular person for whom, as for yourself, marriage is not possible, but you have declared yourselves to each other and the small print has the other's name. It may be a secret commitment. I have known that, and have known the commitment stand despite hopeless circumstances and over-whelming odds. All of us have financial commitments, either to our rents or mortgages or the education of our children or the care of some dependent, on top of our taxes, which we know it is less than Christian to cheat on. "Render to Caesar the things that are Caesar's" are stern words from Christ that still have to be heard and obeyed. No, we are surrounded in our lives by commitments of one kind or another, on top of which and surmounting all as Christians we are expected to be committed to Christ our Savior and Lord. A Christian does not merely subscribe to Christ's ethical teachings out of affection for their beauty.

It is not to a system but to a person — his person, Christ himself, Christ the true and living God — that the claim to be a Christian involves commitment. In the early days of the church, and down to this day, when adults are to be baptized and make their own promises, the question was and is asked of them, "Do you turn to Christ?" And the answer is, "I turn to Christ." To Christ, not to religion. To Christ, not to ethical culture of a sort produced two thousand years ago. To Christ, not to a philosophy of being. Were I not to stress this with everything I have, I could not continue this sermon. Commitment to him is our love life with him, the marriage of our hearts to him. It involves offering him the lot, not merely the best, not merely the most respectable, not merely the strongest in you, not merely the most honorable, but all that and more: the weakness of flesh and will, the capacity for betraying his love, the fears that hold you back from his love, your desire for privacy, for some secret area to be inviolate, the loves you don't wish him to share, the fun you have without him . . . all that and more: what makes you you. "Commit thy way unto the LORD, and put thy trust in him," says the psalmist (Ps. 37:5, BCP). It is only in this setting of putting your *way* — your life's intentions and your life's achievements, your life's disappointments and your life's most private moments — into the loving embrace of Christ that what we hope to do today has any meaning and importance at all.

Consider the people of this world who surround us with one sort of dependency or another — poverty, illiteracy, the weakness of old age, the vulnerability of childhood, addiction to drugs or to alcohol, loneliness whether of bereavement or personality inadequacy. This means the poor, the ignorant, the very old, the very young, the junkie, the drunk, the self-pitying, the boring. Opening ourselves to these people will involve vulnerability on our part to rejection, to distrust, to manipulation, to jealousy. And the like. My question is: are you ready to be open and vulnerable to these things? To ask for patience, and then to have to exercise it with the neurotic? To ask for humility to cope with some uncongenial task, and then find yourself humiliated not once but often in the doing of it for some perhaps ungrateful and demanding recipient? To risk disappointment, and lose your bet? To offer friendship and find it misunderstood, taken advantage of? Because these are possibilities when we consider the rich man. Read the small print — read it knowing that there is no place for do-goodism, no place for patronizing in this work to which we invite you to put your hand. This is God's work among his children whose happiness may depend upon your determination to give of yourself.

There is no shortcut to self-giving for the Christian.

> Jesus, who gave himself for you
> Upon the cross to die,
> Opens to you his Sacred Heart;
> O to that heart draw nigh.

And when you do, you will see very close to that Sacred Heart of love the dependents of the world — the little, the unfortunate, the unlovable, the unsuccessful. It needs determination, not merely kindness, to get close and to stay close to people like that. When Christ tells us about the cup of cold water, it isn't merely our compassion he elicits; it is the effort of will to love and to search out his little ones and be with them as they drink the water, not merely to give them a few cents so they can buy it for themselves. The poor, he says, you will always have with you. They are there, and they won't go away. He identifies with them when he says, "the Son of Man hath not where to lay his head," when he commits himself to them and to us:

> For I was an hungred, and ye gave me meat: I was thirsty, and ye gave me drink: I was a stranger, and ye took me in: naked, and ye clothed me: I was sick, and ye visited me: I was in prison, and ye came unto me. Then shall the righteous answer him saying, Lord, when saw we thee an hungred, and fed thee? or thirsty, and gave thee drink? When saw we thee a stranger, and took thee in? or naked, and clothed thee? Or when saw we thee sick, or in prison, and came unto thee?

And that devastating answer from Christ? "Inasmuch as ye have done it unto one of the least of these my brethren, ye have done it unto me" (Matt. 25:35-40, KJV).

That, my friends, is the majesty and the mystery of the man who is God, the Christ whose faith we own. He requires from us this compassion and commitment toward him in the people who are dependent on us, and today's Gospel is the small print. It may be that you are in fact discovering within yourself the need to practice this, and this is why we have the Community Service Projects Committee, with dedicated members of the parish family running all sorts of enterprises involving people in the life of this city. The priest who is chaplain and friend to all on board is Fr. Stuart Kenworthy. Talk to him. He will be glad to talk to you and will understand if you haven't attempted anything of this kind before. He will refer you. His committee members are committed, and their commitment shows and can inspire yours.

These people, and their needs, are the small print. Commitment to Christ and your commitment to this family of his here in this marvelous church involves reading the small print — the least of these Christ's little ones, for he is there, shining from their eyes and hidden behind their lonely faces and in the touch of their hands.

Seconds Too Late

One of the things we complain about in New York (and with some justification) is the quality of what's appearing on Broadway. Broadway was for years *stupor mundi,* the wonder of the world, with its extraordinary standards of arresting and memorable things to see. Now, good films seem more available to us than good theater. The movies that pull us in, in every sense of that term, are often from and about other countries, *nostalgia films,* if you like, about India — *Passage to India;* about Africa — *Out of Africa;* about England in past days and to do with classes of society with which we are not necessarily familiar — *Room with a View,* the new and fascinating *Maurice, Chariots of Fire, Another Country;* about Russia — *Gorky Park;* about this nation — its war films, its stories of the old South, suspense thrillers like *No Way Out,* farming history. And Australia. Australia, an emerging nation in a decaying Empire, Australia during the first World War. I think of a film some years ago which for spiritual significance and truth came near to tearing me asunder: *Gallipoli.* It was made by Australians about Australians and the part they played in the military operations in the first World War, when the cream of a regiment was sacrificed to murderous Turkish gunfire. Official incompetence and stupidity, miscalculation and arrogance cut into the lives of hundreds of young men

215

with ideals and hopes as high as any to be found the world over. The tragedy of it, the squalid waste that war always brings, tears you apart — and hurts that much more because conceivably it could have been avoided, but the means for avoiding it came seconds too late. Seconds too late.

The tragedy of being just too late — there is much of it in human experience, and in both the Old Testament lesson and the New there are telling evidences of it. You heard how Amos, the herdsman from the tiny village of Tekoa, thundered about this in his warning to the nation of Israel that they might be too late. He had discerned, with all the honesty and frankness of a child, the hollowness of the official religion of his day, tailored to fit its easy adherents, with its shallow optimism, with its power of positive thinking no less, and all the mess that that can get you into (let those with ears to hear, hear), with its assumption that all would work out right in the end if you thought right and your self-image was appropriate, with its tendency to pull God down to size and make him over in our own image, and with its curiously arrogant tendency not to notice anything wrong when you have done so. You think you are ready and you are not. You think you have all the answers sewn up in a bag in your hand, and yet they are not answers, at least not answers to the real questions that real people are asking. You hope for the best without looking the worst in the face. And then, said Amos, the roof will fall in. Listen to him, bearing in mind what I have said about the utter folly of unpreparedness that comes from self-assurance.

> Woe unto you that desire the day of the LORD! to what end is it for you? the day of the LORD is darkness, and not light. As if a man did flee from a lion, and a bear met him; or went into the house, and leaned his hand on the wall, and a serpent bit him. . . . I hate, I despise your feast days, and I will not smell your solemn assemblies . . . neither will I regard the peace

offerings of your fat beasts. . . . Take thou away from me the
noise of thy songs; for I will not hear the melody of thy viols.
But let judgment run down as waters, and righteousness as a
mighty stream.

Amos 5:18-19, 21-24, KJV

What Amos is telling the nation is that they may be
too late. For they are expecting the wrong things, they have
erected false representations of their God and of their destiny
in him. They are concerned about the wrong things. The
prophet is telling them that they have trivialized the things
of God in their preoccupation with a sentimental and cozy
picture of him and of the things he expects from them as
his chosen people. They are playing their own tune when
they should be playing God's. Remember the psalm, "How
shall we sing the Lord's song?"? And God cannot make his
voice heard through the din of their songs and the clamor
of their instruments. They talk in happy terms of final vindication for their nation in the Day of the Lord. God is
talking in terms of judging his people: what have they done
with what they have been given? They see it in terms of
sparkling brightness where they will shine. Amos sees it as
it is under the shadow of God's hand, the hand of the mighty
Lord "whose arm is stretched out still."

Too late, he is saying, too late, too late. You haven't
got it right. For the Day of the Lord, the final day of
reckoning for all nations and all people, will not be "a
breeze," so easy a matter to be got through as not to cause
a moment's worry, when success at the enterprise is assured
and stardom awaits. Between God's final vindication of his
promised, chosen people and *this* side of that consummation
of all things, there is a troubling judgment, all the more
troubling for those who have had the privilege of being
chosen as God's people. That spells darkness, the darkness
of doubt and uncertainty and self-searching, not the sunshine

of presumption, and the people of God cannot see it. It is too late — too late for some, at least.

Our Lord knew Amos's prophecy. He knew it by heart, as all little Jewish boys knew the prophets. He chose a story, the story we heard read in the second lesson. Lamps to be trimmed, oil supplies assured, the discipline of seeing to all these things, no bland assumptions to be made that everything will come out all right in the end, for there is such a thing as accountability when the bridegroom's arrival is spotted. Some will be too late for the kingdom of God. This is no fanciful notion. This is a thread woven through the tapestry of the revelation of God's dealings with us, and Christ restitches it for his church to remember.

He wants us to remember it because there are corporate and individual attitudes to matters of belief that militate against our growing "into the measure of the stature of the fulness of Christ." There are the usual corporate attitudes and epithets for ethnically and politically different groups, and they are usually offensive, unjustifiable, and pejorative as well as ignorant — from kikes to fruitcakes, from broads to lushes, from commies to pigs, and suchlike. Lumped together, they are as ugly as the attitude of superiority that coined them. They are often employed to arouse fear and uncertainty and division. They are terms of scorn, like the word *dogs,* which Jews in Christ's day used in reference to Gentiles. Doubtless Amos had heard that sobriquet, too. The assumption that we are all right, that because we are what we are we have nothing to examine ourselves about, can make us too late for Christ when he comes to us, for what he wants to see is not presumption but penitence, not self-assurance but self-searching, not a hearty welcome but a humble heart. When, years ago, the church formulated the doctrine *extra ecclesiam nulla salus est* ("outside the Church there is no salvation"), it was right in the heavenly way and disastrously wrong in the human way of triumphalism, over-

certainty, and arrogance. For the church militant herself —
which is us, forgiven sinners all — is under the judgment of
God, and we had better not forget it.

Of us to whom much is vouchsafed, much will be
expected. I confess I am sometimes terrified at what the Lord
might be asking of us here, where we have been given so
much, so much architecturally, musically, aesthetically, financially, geographically, where in our parish family we have
devoted self-sacrifice and self-giving in service to others. We
have been blessed with so much. I am terrified at what the
Lord might be asking of us here, terrified that I and you
might be too busy, too involved, too delighted with what
absorbs us to hear the distant song the Lord wants sung,
the real sacrifices he is calling us to make, the deeper holiness
he is looking for, the extra mile he wants us to tread with
those of us who neither understand what we are after in his
name nor approve of what we do. I don't want to be too
late; I don't want my ministry and priesthood among you
to keep you from hearing what he is saying to you through
the eyes of the poor and the unfortunate and the different
and the unsuitable. It is a dread responsibility, and all I can
attempt to tell you is this: there is no place, no place
whatever, for complacency, for self-satisfaction, for comparison with lesser mortals. That is the idleness of the foolish
virgins, the arrogance of the establishment mentality, the
wastefulness of bad and corrupt stewards. What has been
vouchsafed to us is a treasure beyond price, surpassing sterile
morality, a hunger and thirst for righteousness, a heritage
of obedience and hope and acceptance by Christ, who loves
us enough to die for us and defies human history by being
utterly faithful to any promise he has made.

It took the massacre at Gallipoli to bring home to an
obdurate and arrogant colonel the monstrous consequences
of assumptions blandly held, unwillingness to be warned or
to learn the lessons of history. Too late, too late. Our Lord

219

has gentler means of persuasion: his poverty, his humility, his life lived out in the lives of his saints, lamps to see by as clouds and darkness cover the land: "Watch," he says, "and wait!" And of these who have done what he wants?

> These are they *who watched, and waited,*
> offering up to Christ their will;
> Soul and body consecrated,
> day and night they serve him still.
> Now in God's most holy place
> Blest they stand before his face.

The Man Who Came to Dinner

I hope you saw this play at least once in your life. It is very funny. A couple find they are stuck with a stranger who had been invited with a friend of theirs. He stays on. Just as they think finally they can get rid of him, he falls and injures himself, and back into the house he comes, this person they have never known, never met before, never really have wanted in the first place. He was there, and there to stay.

Years ago in my former parish, a young woman was describing to me the resistance put up by her very young son to the arrival of a newborn brother. "I've had to explain gently to him, Father, that his baby brother is here, *and here to stay.*"

When people give Christ houseroom in their hearts, they don't know what they're doing. He has a habit of occupying more rooms than they ever imagined he would want. He likes to be in the dining room, with your friends, enjoying your hospitality. He likes to be at the table when there is no one else there at all and you are planning to eat the leftovers in your T-shirt, unshowered, exhausted from the doings of the day and longing to be free of people and talk. And he likes you to make an effort and talk to him about the terrible day you've had with your workmates and clients and customers who have been more than usually demanding, neurotic, and rude with the New York fiscal crisis looming over them as well as over you. He gently expects you to make an effort. He smiles as you help yourself to a drink and put your feet up in the living room, and he follows you in there to sit on the other side of the fireplace. To your embarrassment he's with you in the shower, washing you down with the soap and drying your feet. All your nakedness, all the extra pounds, the evidence of much-needed but too little self-discipline, all the scars and disfigurements are seen by him, and he makes no comment other than a glance to assure you that they don't embarrass him or cause him to avoid the nearness he has with you.

Of course you'd like to keep him out of the bedroom, especially if you have company, and even more so, perhaps, if you have a spouse. "Is no place sacred?" you say to yourself. He's even in here, too near to the bed. He's hearing what I'm saying, and he's smiling in enjoyment. He's getting no kicks out of being there. He's just there, when you are licitly or illicitly enjoying yourself. The man to whom you've given houseroom is *everywhere* in your life — at your side at the bank counter, looking over your shoulder as you write that nasty or anonymous letter, sitting looking sad as you score a cruel point in a row with someone you love, his reflection in the glass you drink to drown your sorrows and forget it all. It's curiously hard to see where he is when you are being hypocritical, or vengeful, or pushy, or jealous, and he's never a support when you enjoy getting angry.

Allow Christ houseroom, and you don't know what you are in for. Strangely, the people we identify as saints don't seem to care whether they know what they are in for. On the whole they seem devil-may-care to the possibilities of regret, although it is true that some of them give evidence of occasional twinges of resentment at his occupancy. But mostly they have a sense that they must make room for someone they suspect has been loving them a lot longer than they have loved him. Did not somebody once say that "we love because he loved us first" (1 John 4:19, NEB)? My guess — and it's a guess no shrewder than yours — is that they have a flash of insight into the necessity for *gratitude* to a loving God. Look at the saints you know about. All of them seem to be curiously *grateful*. Grateful to God for making them and all of us in his image. Grateful for such love he has for the world that he gave us "his only begotten Son, that whosoever believeth in him should not perish, but have everlasting life" (John 3:16, KJV). Grateful for that unbelievable generosity and self-giving, that divine foolishness, that heavenly prodigality, and realizing that generosity on our part is the natural reaction, the supernatural requirement, that hospitality to Christ is the order of the day and the key to our destiny.

Today is the day when we gather to give thanks to God for all those souls who in gratitude to that self-giving God have offered Christ houseroom, only to find that he has come to occupy everything that makes them them, that he has gone from being a guest, the man who came to dinner, to being a companion homemaker who occupies on condition of their willing surrender the private chambers of their hearts. He has rearranged their furniture, so things are not quite what they were. But he has also given them a new eye to help them see things differently, and they appreciate the change. These are the saints, a bewilderingly diverse crowd from every nation under heaven, each one surprised to hear the title, totally unaware of difference between themselves and us, all unselfconsciously placing Christ first in their lives and allowing him to do the talking. Through them we become aware of him as he shines through their eyes and makes his presence felt in the way they do things.

Not that they are paragons of virtue. It takes a cold-hearted, self-conscious, calculating climber to be a paragon. Saints have faults, often alarmingly obvious and occasionally intensely irritating to the more efficient and self-sufficient of us. They can be silly and misled and at times unreasonable. But there is a curious family likeness, a cast of countenance, if you will. For whatever reason, they make Christ's reality alive to us.

Talking of which, today is a Sunday assigned by the church for public baptism. In a few moments three babies and two adults will be baptized in front of you. St. Paul uses a strange phrase: "Baptized into union with him, you have all *put on Christ as a garment*" (Gal. 3:27, NEB).

Isn't that another way of saying the sort of thing that saints have done so magnificently in giving Christ houseroom — putting Christ on like a garment? We are here to witness five of God's children take the first step in response to God's will and wish for their lives to make room for Christ, to give him houseroom, to put Christ on as a garment.

When Paul addresses the members of the church at Corinth as people "called to be saints" (1 Cor. 1:2, RSV) he is using the phrase just like this, describing people responding to God's wish for them to give Christ houseroom. It is that which makes them different from (not superior to) the people who have no time for that sort of thing. It is giving Christ a chance to rearrange the furniture in their lives, and being happy with the changes he makes — even if the armchairs are a little less comfortable so that our selfish ease is not so easily accommodated, even if the rooms are a little more drafty so that we feel more keenly the pains and wants and discomforts of many other of God's people in the world, even if the windows are left open to receive the winds of the Spirit, even if there are fewer mirrors around to admire ourselves in, even if the beds are a little less inviting as places in which to exercise our lusts and our laziness. And Christ is everywhere, wherever we go, for time and for eternity.

Appointment with Fear

When I was a boy there was a weekly thriller on the BBC that would make me glue a horrified ear to the radio. Its title was to a youngster bloodchilling, and the announcer made it more so: *Appointment with Fear*. It is about time we said something about fear in this city. I was put in mind of this when a letter from two beloved parishioners arrived that read like this:

> Yesterday, New York City showed us its ugly side again. It started at the Tunnel entrance with a confrontation of the car ahead with the authorities, people shouting and police running, etc. At the other end, the "willy-nilly windshield brigade" swarmed over our car for the weekly contest of wills (and the ever-present threat of violence). Recent visits have seen people shooting up on the very steps of the church, a woman assaulted in front at Evensong time, and ever-growing tension among even hardened New Yorkers. Some time ago we were able to abort an attack on us by turning suddenly and confronting the would-be perpetrators, who promptly ran away. . . . We've decided to cut back our visits to once a month. We simply can't do without St. Thomas entirely, although our friends . . . think us brave indeed to venture into the city at all.

The parable of fear was taken up by the Cardinal Archbishop of New York when our Bishop Grein and I were at lunch with him a few days ago. The fear isn't confined to the violence that my parish family mention in the letter. It's not confined to the young men who insist on washing the windshield of your car, nor to the altercation at the mouth of the Tunnel, nor to the appalling treatment of women and men in the course of robbery, nor to the families of children caught in crossfire and killed by stray bullets. It is the fear that somehow the city is crumbling into the rubble of a battleground, where there is no safe place, no haven, no atmosphere of peace, no trust, no future.

Some of you heard Tony Guida on the Channel 4 news at 6 o'clock on Friday, when we were treated to appalling reports of angry accusations and frustration and violence as the *Daily News* began to tumble into what looked like its death throes, that he had for a long time worked with many of the writers on the newspaper, and he hardly dared look into their faces for the fear he saw written on them. Fear of violence. Fear of unemployment. Fear for family impoverishment. Fear of enforced idleness. Fear for the weekly bills that would perforce have to go unpaid. Fear for what the future holds for this city itself, as unhappy and bruised and battered as it is with every possible ill assailing it.

There is fear on every side. This city is wrapped in it. At least it seems so. Now we have the Hasidim in a tussle with the Hispanics, and violence inside our police headquarters as screaming hordes belabor the police. Defendants in the jogger trial scream at the judges and their own lawyers. The lawyers scream at the judge. All inhibition is thrown aside as people get into the fight. I suspect fear lies at the bottom of much of this unbridled behavior. I have talked about this before, but I think this particular nail needs another hammering.

When trouble is brewing and danger looms, who can shrug it off? Some people cope with its approach better than others. Some people panic miserably. Some have fears that are imaginary — the psalmist speaks of them: "They were afraid where no fear was." Others cloak their cowardice with expressions of concern. Do you remember the screams and rage when in 1985 the Roman Catholic Archdiocese bravely wished to make one of its disused properties into a hospice for sufferers from AIDS? Do you remember how the screamers in that neighborhood won? I wonder if they really faced their consciences before they shouted the proposal down. What do you think the doctors and nurses feel like when people yell like that? What is a little child infected with AIDS to feel like when his companions are kept away from him, when no school will take him, when no friends will play with him? In the face of this particular danger, if you see it as a danger, where would you put yourself? Where would you put your children?

Wherever we look, it seems, danger walks the streets of this city dealing death and deprivation by injury or robbery to the people who venture on them, as I can very well attest. I must confess that I am conscious of the existence of it, though it doesn't deter me from leaving the safety of my home to go to somebody else's of an evening. Life has to go on even though an enjoyable stroll alone is no longer as safe as once it was. But then think about parts of Ireland or the West Bank in Israel. Nobody feels safe anymore.

The wish for safety is primeval. There is an ancient, deep-down nostalgia for safety. Animals choose their place of sleep instinctively with an eye to flight. Erecting walls has been a pastime since Jericho, long before Winston Churchill popularized bricklaying. Go to the Yucatan, explore stone-age cave dwellings. Wherever people choose to live, they try to make it safe with walls, with ramparts, with moats, with ditches.

We are a worried civilization. The things that have brought us convenience have brought us anxiety. There is danger in airplane travel. There is danger in car travel. There is danger in the use of electrical appliances. There is danger in medical discoveries. There is danger in speed. But we simply have to risk the dangers inherent in all these things with which we live our contemporary lives if we want to get from one place to another, and eat, and enjoy the healing process in body and mind and the possibilities for a fuller life.

Remember that psalm I quoted: "They were afraid where no fear was." That is not only an imagined danger. It is an unworthy fear.

To refuse to come to terms with life because of its inherent dangers is to live in fear, and fear is a paralyzing force that reduces not only our activities but our horizons. Think of judgments arrived at in fear. They are cruel. They are self-serving. They punish other people by shutting them out or locking them in. Racial discrimination is one of the evil fruits of fear. The Hitlerite myth of Aryan superiority bred destruction for millions of Christ's own race, and we know that fear lay at the bottom of it. Whatever the arguments are about the Republic of South Africa's management of its affairs, it is undeniable that fear is to be discovered stooping under the tables in the houses of its people and under the desks of legislators. We have only to look at what motivates the Ku Klux Klan or political parties devoted to racial purity in this country; I have only to look at the National Front policies in Britain and the bloody riots there between ethnic groups. And fear rules in totalitarian states, dictating policies and preparing defenses.

But what are the dangers in your own life that cause you to fear, those dangers apart from the dangers of daily living that at one time or other worry us all?

Is there a danger that you will be left alone, abandoned through death by the person in your life around whom a lot of it centers? Is there a danger that an illness you have may leave you disabled, imprisoning you in your house or in your chair or in your bed? Is there a danger that you may be disapproved of for something that you are or have done, that friends will no longer count you as one, a family will reject you, or an enemy will take advantage of you? Is there a danger that you could fail in an enterprise upon which you have set your heart? Fears of one sort or another in response to dangers of one sort or another are the daily bread of not a few whom you pass on the sidewalk or rub shoulders with in the subway or even sit next to in the pew. Horizons are reduced for many and initiative is crippled for many by these fears.

What has the church and Scripture to say to people who are frightened, whose lives are paralyzed by fears stemming from greater or lesser dangers? In the first place, Christ has three things to say:

1. "Do not be afraid of them. There is nothing covered up that will not be uncovered, nothing hidden that will not be made known" (Matt. 10:26, NEB).
2. "Do not fear those who kill the body, but cannot kill the soul. Fear him rather who is able to destroy both soul and body in hell" (Matt. 10:28, NEB).
3. "Are not sparrows two a penny? Yet without your Father's leave not one of them can fall to the ground. As for you, even the hairs of your head have all been counted. So have no fear; you are worth more than any number of sparrows" (Matt. 10:29-31, NEB).

Three times in almost as many verses Christ talks to release us from fears of danger. The things covered that will be uncovered, the things hidden that will be made known are the things of truth. Truth will triumph. When a Scottish king sought to threaten a man with execution or exile, the man replied, "You cannot hang or exile the truth!" That defiant answer has echoed through the arches of history. Truth will prevail. Why will truth prevail? I'll tell you why truth will prevail. Christ it is who says, "I am the truth."

Second, Christ says that nothing by way of retribution meted out by human beings need be feared compared with the fate that awaits a soul that has recognized God for who he is and then deliberately turned away in scorn, rejecting God. It is not God's affront so much as his *absence* that can kill a man's soul. "It is a fearful thing to fall into the hands of the living God"; we might well add that it is a fearful thing to fall *out* of the hands of the living God. The fear of God of which Christ speaks is not a craven fear but a sense of awe and wonder — a holy fear, the profoundest respect, in which love has a genuine part. That fear is healthy.

Third, Christ is pointing out with a telling comparison to the the cost of a sparrow the worth to God of a human soul. Sparrows were bought for half a penny. St. Luke in recording this incident actually makes the deal better. Are not *five* sparrows sold for two pennies? The fifth sparrow was thrown in for free. And yet their place in the scheme of things is in God's hands — and we are worth more, much more, than a sparrow, for we are made in the image of God. What happens to us is not outside the awareness of God, and it is for that reason that we should not give in to fear.

This is bracing reassurance from the Savior himself — that truth will prevail, that only the scornful rejection of God constitutes grounds for fear, that the individual soul and body are precious to the Creator.

John, who knew this teaching, brings insights of his own. In his first letter he writes, "there is no room for fear in love; perfect love banishes fear. For fear brings with it the pain of judgement, and anyone who is afraid has not attained to love in its perfection. We love because he loved us first" (1 John 4:18-19, NEB). This is armor of the finest steel, the steel of which the sword of the spirit is forged. That armor is not easily manufactured, and in fact it is impossible for us to make it. It is only on God's anvil that such armor is made, and the fire in which it is forged is the fire of his love. We need that armor. We know where to get it. We know who makes it in our size, to fit us, for time and for eternity.

King Alfred, the one who burned the cakes, remember? — it was he who said, "If you have a fearful thought, share it not with a weakling; whisper it to your saddle-bow, and ride forth singing!"

For Leslie Lang
February 5, 1909–April 26, 1990

An unwanted priest has a heavy spiritual burden to bear, especially if his priesthood has been regarded as influential and effective. Leslie John Alden Lang was carrying that burden on his back when in 1974 I discovered him sitting in the pews of this church. He had been required to retire, and he was humiliated and hurt by the reasons for it, which may well have sounded sense but which were insensitive also. This stalwart, craggy convert from Massachusetts Congregationalism had been the Catholic support and encourager and mentor of the dashing young Horace Donegan on his becoming the Twelfth Bishop of New York — this after close years with his predecessor Bishop Manning, whose Catholic leadership was well known, respected, and resented. It is known by many of us that Leslie's influence on Horace Donegan's episcopate brought to life and light a Catholic awareness to the flair for the dramatic that the bishop possessed, and Leslie's intellectual input helped in the theological development of that beloved and effective father in God whose years in this city and diocese made many clergy and laypeople happy and effective also. It was, in Leslie's words, "a golden time."

But Leslie, for all his memories — and they were inexhaustible and accurate and on occasions hilarious — was never one for leaning back on the silken pillows of nostalgia.

232

He could have been the archetypal ecclesiastical club bore recounting how things were *when*. . . . But he wasn't. He lived firmly in the present, thanking God fervently for opportunities to press home the truths of the Catholic faith as they presented themselves, seeing chinks of light in foggy situations. Without sentimentality, without visible excitement, in a pace of voice like the speed of a great ship coming into port, he would say what he saw, and say it briefly. He was the despair of the garrulous. He disappointed the gossips. He knew more than he told. He released insights in situations where they might help, and he prayed for wisdom. God richly answered that prayer. We had in our midst a grave, joyful figure of immense and unselfconscious dignity, with no tricks of speech or idiosyncrasy to draw attention to himself. His recollection and peace at the altar of God attested to that. To see him walk in procession, in his simplicity, his hands held in happy prayerful relaxation, his face at peace, was a lesson. His beautiful voice reading the Scriptures, offering the sacrifice of the mass, deep, deliberate, with his New England ancestry making itself evident in its power and clarity, was a gift to us. He was very near to the unseen God, whom he knew better than he let us know. His discretion was a clue to this, as was his charity.

Leslie had a great capacity for friendship, often unusual. Friends came into his life and stayed. Decades of companionship with Fr. Tom Brown and Bishop Donegan and with his juniors whom I join today can attest to it. I feel I have never known the time when he was not in my life, a confession Fr. Jay Gordon or Fr. Edgar Wells, to name but two, might also make. And at this point his young friend Michael Javelos, who looked after him in the last months and days, should be remembered with gratitude.

I would stand in the sacristy during the sixteen years he was here at St. Thomas and watch young curates pull his leg and give him no peace. He loved them equally and gave

233

as good as he got. He taught us all with a gift for preaching that he never thought he had until he came here. Something in this place triggered it, as he often acknowledged to me quietly. He preached powerfully. He converted souls. He strengthened the faith of parishioners and priests alike. His friendship, which we all cherished, made us happy to listen to his incisive faith humorously and sensitively passed on. It had been hammered out on the anvil of time and tested, and we knew it was authentic.

He was no feminist, that's for sure. But his many close women friends would hasten to say that he was no sexist either. They loved him dearly, and undemonstratively and generously he loved them back. The point is that all of us through our love for him learned a lot from him, and we are all the beneficiaries of his capacity to be our friend.

We all knew he liked his bourbon and a decent companionable dinner with congenial conversation. He was a good team player at the table, and when he told his stories, often self-deprecating, sometimes surprising, there was much laughter, and we would catch another side of him and of the situation he would describe. Through our memories of Leslie were countless occasions of *sitting*. He was a good sitter. His own relaxation made itself available to a group of people, regardless of the context — in an Anglican–Roman Catholic discussion of the two jurisdictions of which he was a valued member, or when he was stating his hopes for the health of our church and its future despite all evidences to the contrary, or in some clerical group or other, or in the houses of his friends. He brought charity and sanity *and salt* so that we wanted to do better and think better and forgive more easily and see more clearly.

What a man! What a priest! What a brother to *Virginia!* What a history of loving service given to this diocese. Ordained priest in 1934 by Bishop Sherrill, he served in St. Peter's parish in Westchester as curate and rector from 1934 to 1963, with a short break in between. Then the intercession, and finally sixteen years in this place. I don't want to claim more than is right, but he often spoke of his deep and abiding happiness here as the crown of his priestly self-oblation.

Let it be said publicly that the coming of †Richard Grein to be our new father in God was the source of much comfort and encouragement to him, and he often told me so.

We watched him lose flesh and become frail. I and others begged him to see a doctor, and when he finally did, he came back quietly with the news of his cancer. We shielded him from the alarm we shared as best we could, and he rarely made mention of his discomfort, even saying that he found his condition "very interesting." So to that life of faith and serene proclamation was added the dimension of patience and courage in much suffering. He embraced it and worked until he physically dropped, as he had said he intended to do. When last Thursday Michael told me that the doors of death were opened to Leslie, I was able to be with him for the last moments of his life. I read the Prayers for the Dying and the old Commendation of the Soul, and he died at the Amen. Exactly and typically was this Leslie's way of cooperating with God and the things of God's world.

From us he has returned to God, a strong example, a model, no less, of priesthood and faithful self-giving, a long life of friendships and joyful associations. Leslie, you are now completely well and better as you walk toward the Lord whose priesthood you shared and whom you loved so much, who greets you and bids you pray for us as now we pray for you.